Oxford Discover

Workbook 4

Kathleen Kampa
Charles Vilina

OXFORD
UNIVERSITY PRESS

BIG QUESTION 1

Where are we in the universe?

Think and write.

What do you know?

____

____

____

____

____

____

____

____

What do you want to know?

____

____

____

____

____

____

____

____

UNIT 1 Get Ready

Words

A Read and write.

moon asteroids comet ~~stars~~

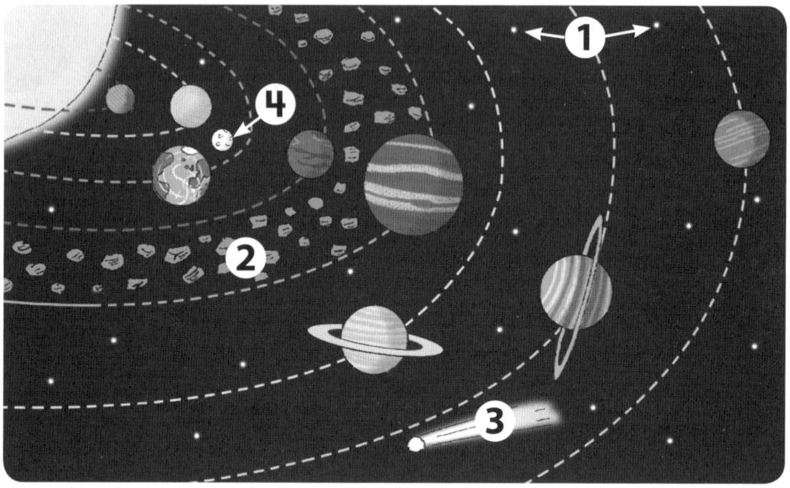

1 stars

3 ________

2 ________

4 ________

B Read and circle the correct answer.

1 You can use this to look at stars.

a moon **b** telescope **c** galaxy

2 This can take you away from Earth.

a spacecraft **b** comet **c** meteorite

3 This is a place where you can look at objects in the night sky.

a meteorite **b** universe **c** observatory

4 This is all of space, including the solar system and billions of galaxies.

a asteroids **b** comet **c** universe

5 This is a rock that falls to Earth from space.

a comet **b** meteorite **c** galaxy

C Circle True (T) or False (F).

1	A galaxy has many stars in it.	(T)	F
2	Use a telescope to look at things close to you.	T	F
3	Earth has more than one moon.	T	F
4	Astronauts travel in a spacecraft.	T	F
5	There are meteorites on Earth.	T	F
6	The universe has many galaxies in it.	T	F
7	An asteroid is made of gas.	T	F
8	An observatory is for studying plants.	T	F
9	The sun is a star.	T	F
10	A comet moves through space.	T	F
11	Our solar system has only one planet.	T	F

D Read the paragraph. Complete the sentences with the words in the box.

telescope	spacecraft	observatory	~~universe~~	meteorite

Marco wanted to be an astronaut someday and travel though the **universe** (1) in a ________ (2). One day, Marco found a large, shiny, black stone in the park. He showed it to his father, who is a scientist. His father said that the stone could be a ________ (3). He asked Marco to bring the stone to the ________ (4) where Marco's father worked every night. "We'll show it to the other scientists," he said. "You can also look through the ________ (5) there." Marco was excited.

Read

A Read. What does Stanley do with George and Amanda?

____

____

B Read again. Remember to make pictures in your mind. Think about how these pictures change as you read.

Stanley's Super Spacecraft

In the year 2099, every child on Earth had his or her own **spacecraft**. Of course, they were small and couldn't travel out of the **solar system**. This was fine for everyone except Stanley. He was curious about the whole universe, so he worked on his spacecraft until it could go anywhere!

His friends, George and Amanda, were not excited about Stanley's super spacecraft.

"Who wants to see the **universe**?" George asked. "Our solar system is big enough."

"That's true," agreed Amanda. "Yesterday I went shopping on Mars and then flew around some **asteroids** for fun. I even chased a **comet**."

"Just hop in," said Stanley. "Today I will take you on an amazing journey."

They got into Stanley's spacecraft. Soon the three friends were flying past the **moon**.

"Now, watch this," said Stanley. He pushed a red button.

Whoosh! went the spacecraft. George and Amanda grabbed their seats tightly and looked out the window. The sun was just a speck of light. Around it were billions of **stars** in the shape of a disk.

"That's our Milky Way **galaxy**," said Stanley. He pressed a blue button.

Whoooooosh! The spacecraft flew farther into space. Suddenly they saw billions of tiny galaxies all around them.

"Welcome to the universe," said Stanley.

Think
Describe the pictures in your mind of the solar system and Milky Way galaxy.

Amanda gasped. "I will remember this day forever. Thank you, Stanley."

"It's amazing, Stanley. Thank you," George said. "Can we stop at the moon for a pizza on our way back? I'm really hungry."

"Of course!" said Stanley. His super spacecraft raced back to the moon.

Think
Describe how the pictures in your mind changed as you read the story.

Comprehension

A Do you think Stanley's story could be true someday? Why or why not?

____

____

B How did the pictures change in your mind as Stanley flew further from Earth? Write in the chart.

First	Next	Finally
Earth was a beautiful blue ball behind Stanley's spacecraft.		

C Answer the questions.

1 Do George and Amanda have their own spacecraft? How do you know?

____

____

2 What did Amanda do the day before she flew with Stanley?

____

3 How did Amanda feel about her day in Stanley's spacecraft? Why do you think she felt that way?

____

____

D **Words in Context** Read and write.

vast	dwell	specks	disk

1 Most stars seem like ____________ of light.

2 There is nothing more ____________ than the universe.

3 The Milky Way is shaped like a ____________ .

4 Astronauts travel through space, but they ____________ on Earth.

Grammar in Use

A Study the grammar.

Learn **Predictions with *Will***

I **will** take you on an amazing journey.

Amanda **will** remember this day forever.

She'll want to go on another adventure with Stanley.

They'll go even further into space the next time they travel.

she'll = she will   they'll = they will

B **Underline the word *will* in each sentence. Circle the verb after it. Then match.**

1 My little brother says he will be the first person to walk on Mars.

2 Astronauts will find water on a planet someday.

3 Another bright comet will appear in the sky sometime soon.

4 Each child will have his or her own spacecraft in the future.

5 Students will take field trips to the moon someday.

6 Scientists will build even bigger telescopes in the future.

[ ] **a**

[ ] **b**

[1] **c**

[ ] **d**

[ ] **e**

[ ] **f**

C Complete the sentences using *will* and the verbs in the box.

let take fly ~~travel~~ invent wear

1 Astronauts **will travel** to other planets in our solar system someday.

2 Scientists ________________ a spacecraft that can travel outside of our solar system.

3 Bigger telescopes ________________ us look deeper into space.

4 Spacecraft ________________ through space at very high speeds.

5 People ________________ trips to the moon as tourists someday.

6 Astronauts ________________ lighter spacesuits so they can move easily.

D Read. Then write *P* (prediction) or *F* (fact).

1 Someday people will fly to other planets in spacecraft. **P**

2 The sun will rise tomorrow morning at 6:30. _____

3 Scientists will build a city on the moon in the future. _____

4 Space tours will take people to the moon and back. _____

5 There will be a full moon this month. _____

E Unscramble the sentences.

1 system / fly / will / the / People / spacecraft / through / solar

People will fly spacecraft through the solar system.

2 through / will / Astronauts / universe / the / travel

____

3 will / ground / meteorites / hit / Small / the / tonight

____

4 fast / will / someday / Spacecraft / fly / very

____

Communicate

Word Study

sleigh	veil	reins	freight	weigh	eighty

A Read each sentence. Circle the words with *ei* that have a *long a* sound. Then match.

1 Leah received a beautiful red sleigh for her birthday.

2 The new telescope at school is over eighty kilograms, so you can't lift it.

3 In the future, spacecraft may deliver freight to other planets.

4 The young woman wore a beautiful white veil on her head.

5 Esteban grabbed the reins and rode his horse through the rain.

6 Space observatories don't weigh anything once they are in space.

a

b

c

d

e

f

B Complete the sentences with the words in the box.

I saw an old photo of a Finnish man and his wife going to town on a large ____(1) carrying ____(2) chickens in cages. Two large horses pulled it. The man had the ____(3) in his hand, and the horses were moving quickly through the snow. The chickens probably did not ____(4) very much. I think the horses seemed happy to be pulling such light ____(5) .

Writing Study

A **Read. Underline the sentence that's incomplete. Then rewrite it to make it complete.**

1 Sirius is a very bright star. Can see it easily in the night sky. It is also called the Dog Star.

You can see it easily in the night sky.

2 The universe is vast. Difficult to imagine. It would take 100,000 years just to travel through the Milky Way galaxy at the speed of light.

3 Look up at the sky. Do you see that bright shiny object? It's a comet! Large icy object.

4 My little brother, Jason, said he will go to the moon someday. Told me last night. He thinks the moon is made of cheese, and Jason loves to eat cheese!

B **Read the text. Then write a paragraph about an object in the universe. Write at least one prediction using *will*. Be sure to write complete sentences.**

Asteroids are usually far away from Earth. They travel around the sun like planets. What do asteroids look like? They come in many shapes and sizes. Some look like giant potatoes! **Scientists will send astronauts to an asteroid someday.**

Student Book page 15

Get Ready

Words

A Decode the words.

astronomer   space probe   ~~core~~   gravity   orbit   matter
diameter   unique   surface   craters   distance

a	b	c	d	e	f	g	h	i	j	k	l	m	n	o	p	q	r	s	t	u	v	w	x	y	z
1	2	3	4	5	6	7	8	9	10	11	12	13	14	15	16	17	18	19	20	21	22	23	24	25	26

1 c o r e
3 15 18 5

2 ___ ___ ___ ___ ___   ___ ___ ___ ___ ___
19 16 1 3 5   16 18 15 2 5

3 ___ ___ ___ ___ ___ ___ ___
7 18 1 22 9 20 25

4 ___ ___ ___ ___ ___ ___ ___ ___ ___ ___
1 19 20 18 15 14 15 13 5 18

5 ___ ___ ___ ___ ___ ___
21 14 9 17 21 5

6 ___ ___ ___ ___ ___ ___ ___ ___
4 9 19 20 1 14 3 5

7 ___ ___ ___ ___ ___ ___ ___
19 21 18 6 1 3 5

8 ___ ___ ___ ___ ___ ___
13 1 20 20 5 18

9 ___ ___ ___ ___ ___ ___ ___ ___
4 9 1 13 5 20 5 18

10 ___ ___ ___ ___ ___ ___ ___
3 18 1 20 5 18 19

11 ___ ___ ___ ___ ___
15 18 2 9 20

B Read and number.

1 orbit   **2** surface   **3** astronomer   **4** craters
5 core   **6** space probe   **7** diameter   **8** distance

☐ 

☐ 

☐ 

☐ 

☐ 

☐ 

☐ 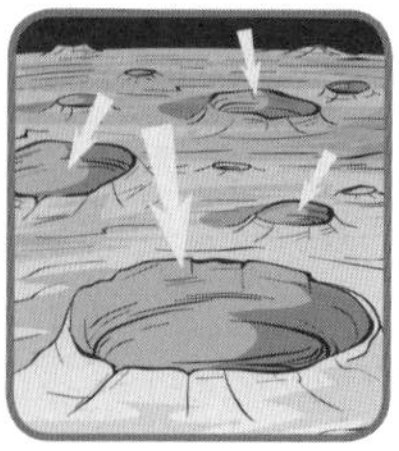

☐ 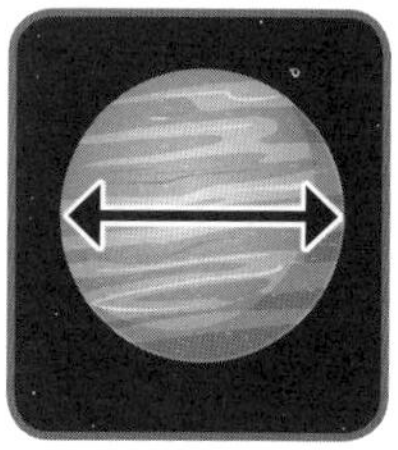

C Circle the correct word to complete each sentence.

1 Our Earth is one example of **distance** / **matter** / **astronomer** in the universe.

2 Every planet in the solar system is **diameter** / **core** / **unique** .

3 We couldn't stand on the ground without **gravity** / **craters** / **orbit** .

D Complete the sentences using the words in the box.

astronomer	space probes	core	gravity	orbit	matter
diameters	unique	surface	craters	distance	

1 With a telescope, you can easily see ________________ on the moon.

2 An ________________ knows a lot of information about the solar system.

3 The moon has weaker ________________ than Earth, so astronauts weigh less there.

4 It takes Earth one year to complete one ________________ around the sun.

5 Earth and Venus are close in size. They have similar ________________ .

6 The ________________ from Earth to the moon is about 384,000 kilometers.

7 ________________ travel through space and send information to Earth.

8 The moon's ________________ is very gray, rocky, and full of craters.

9 The sun has most of the ________________ in the solar system.

10 It is very hot in Earth's ________________ .

11 Each planet in the solar system is ________________ in different ways.

Read

A Read. What makes Ganymede special?

B Read again. How are Ganymede and Earth's moon alike and different?

Ganymede, Jupiter's Giant Moon

Earth has only one moon. It moves in an **orbit** around our planet. It often shines brightly in the night sky. However, did you know that the planet Jupiter has 49 moons? Ganymede is Jupiter's largest moon.

Ganymede is also the largest moon in the solar system. Earth's moon is the fifth largest moon in the solar system. Ganymede's **diameter** is much larger than our moon's diameter. Also, Ganymede is quite far from Jupiter. Earth's moon is closer to Earth. Ganymede goes around Jupiter in just seven days. Earth's moon goes around Earth in 27 days.

Galileo was a famous **astronomer**. He discovered Ganymede in 1610. Today, we understand much more about this giant moon. The Pioneer 10 **space probe** gave us good information about Ganymede. The Voyager and Galileo space probes gave us more information. Scientists now know that Ganymede has rocks and ice. Its **surface** has **craters** like Earth's moon. The **core** of Ganymede is hot and made of metal. The core of Earth's moon is similar. Some scientists think that Ganymede has an ocean. It is 200 kilometers below the surface. Earth's moon has no ocean.

Think
How are Ganymede and our moon different?

Astronauts walked on Earth's moon. However, they can't walk on Ganymede yet. It is too far away. If astronauts go to Ganymede someday, they will be able to jump very high. The gravity on Ganymede is like the gravity on Earth's moon. Scientists know a lot about Ganymede. However, they hope to learn more in the future.

Think
How are Ganymede and our moon alike?

Student Book page 17

Comprehension

A What is one interesting thing you learned about Ganymede?

____

____

B How are the two moons below alike and different? Write.

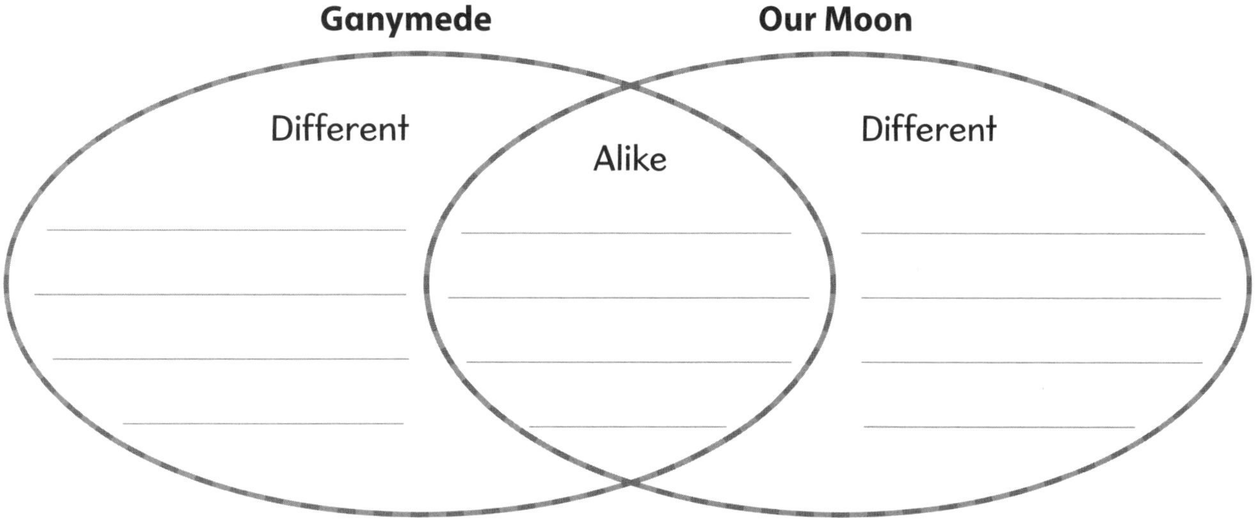

C Circle True (T) or False (F).

1 Ganymede has a larger diameter than Earth's moon. T F

2 The core of Earth's moon is icy and cold. T F

3 Ganymede moves faster through space than Earth's moon. T F

4 Ganymede's gravity is stronger than Earth's gravity. T F

D **Words in Context** Read and write.

explored	bodies	inner	outer

1 Asteroids are ______________ that orbit the sun between Mars and Jupiter.

2 Planets in the ______________ part of the solar system are much colder than Earth.

3 The ______________ planets are smaller than Jupiter and Saturn.

4 The students ______________ the observatory with their teacher and the astronomer.

Grammar in Use

A Study the grammar.

Learn **Future Real Conditional**

If he	**becomes** **doesn't become**	an astronaut, he	**will explore** **won't explore**	the solar system.	
They	**will fail** **won't fail**	the astronomy test if they	**don't study** **study**	hard.	
If I	**don't repair** **repair**	the telescope, I	**won't be able to see** **will be able to see**	Ganymede.	

If the sky **is** clear, **will** she **go** to the observatory? Yes, she **will**.
Will she **go** to the observatory if the sky **isn't** clear? No, she **won't**.

What **will** he **see** if he **looks** at the sky?
If he **looks** at the sky, what **will** he **see**? **He'll see** the moon.

won't = will not

B Read each sentence. Underline what may happen in the future. Circle what will happen as a result.

1 If scientists continue to study Ganymede, they will learn much more about it.
2 If scientists don't find water on Ganymede, they will be disappointed.
3 People will travel through the solar system if we create fast spacecraft.
4 Kenan will build a model solar system if he finds the right materials.
5 If Jackie doesn't finish her homework, she won't use her telescope tonight.
6 If the space probe continues at this speed, it will fly by Ganymede next month.
7 The large meteorite will make a big crater if it hits the moon.
8 If the sky is clear tonight, we will see Venus, Mars, and Jupiter.

C Match.

1 Where will astronauts go first •
2 If astronauts find water on Ganymede someday, •
3 Where will the space probe be in one year •
4 If we go to an observatory, •

• **a** what will you look at through the telescope?
• **b** if they can travel outside of the solar system?
• **c** will they be able to drink it?
• **d** if it continues at this speed?

D Write future real conditional sentences. Use *you* as the subject.

1 not study science / not become an astronaut

If you don't study science, you won't become an astronaut.

2 look at the sky tonight / see Venus and Mars

____

3 read about Ganymede / learn many interesting facts

____

4 not look through the telescope / miss seeing Jupiter's moons

____

E Answer the questions. Write future real conditional sentences.

1 If the sky is clear tonight, which planet will you look for?

If the sky is clear tonight, I will look for Venus in the western sky.

2 What will you do if it rains this weekend?

____

____

3 If you have a test next week, what will you do the day before?

____

____

4 What will your parents do if you get good grades this month?

____

____

Word Study

ignorance	fragrant	arrogant	fragrance	ignorant	arrogance

A Read each sentence. Circle *-ance* or *-ant*. Then match.

1 After she won the race, her arrogance was really bad.

2 Some flowers are very fragrant, while others are not.

3 Tom studies a lot because he doesn't want to be ignorant.

4 An orange tree in the spring can have a lovely fragrance.

5 He acted arrogant, and his friends didn't like it.

6 Ignorance can cause low scores at school.

a

b

c

d

e

f

B Complete the sentences using the words in the box.

1 I smelled the wonderful ____________ of the hot apple pie.

2 Beth doesn't want to be ____________. She is always learning.

3 A rose garden can be very ____________ in the summer.

4 The soccer player is so ____________. He thinks he's the best.

5 If you don't want to have ____________, study hard.

6 The movie star's ____________ made people not like him.

Writing Study

A **Circle the word *or* in each sentence. Underline the choices. Then answer the questions.**

1 Is a galaxy a star or a group of stars?

A galaxy is a group of stars.

2 Is Ganymede's orbit around Mars or Jupiter?

3 Does a moon go around a planet, or does a planet go around a moon?

4 Does our solar system have seven planets or eight planets?

B **Read. Then write a paragraph about exploring the universe. Use at least one choice question and at least one future real conditional sentence in your writing.**

Should astronauts explore the solar system, or should space probes explore it? Space probes don't need food or oxygen to give us information about planets. **If we have better technology someday, we will send people to other planets.** For now, space probes are an easier way to get information.

Wrap Up

Writing

A Read this compare and contrast report about an imaginary solar system. Label the parts of the report.

The V-18 Solar System

In my imagination, I took a trip in my spacecraft to the V-18 Solar System in the Misty Galaxy. I discovered that V-18 is similar to our solar system in some ways but different in other ways.

V-18 is similar to our solar system in three ways. First, its sun is a yellow star that is the same size as our sun. Next, like our solar system, some of the planets have moons, and some don't. Also, one of the planets has rings just like Saturn.

My imaginary solar system is also different from our solar system in three ways. To start with, it has nine inner planets and nine outer planets. Next, the planets Alpha and Beta have plants and animals on them, but no people. Finally, Alpha and Beta go around the sun every 100 days.

I really enjoyed visiting my imaginary solar system. If I have a spaceship someday, I will explore a real solar system. I would love to explore our solar system or one like V-18.

B Plan your imaginary solar system. Include the name of your solar system and galaxy and the number of planets. Then add details in the Venn diagram.

Imaginary Solar System **Earth's Solar System**

Different

Alike

Different

C Now go to your notebook to write your own compare and contrast report. Then read and revise it.

My writing checklist:

- ☐ I included an interesting idea in the introduction paragraph.
- ☐ I wrote about similarities in the second paragraph.
- ☐ I wrote about differences in the third paragraph.
- ☐ I included an interesting idea in the conclusion paragraph.

Student Book pages 24–25

What did you learn?

BIG QUESTION 1

Where are we in the universe?

Review

A **Complete the puzzle.**

Across →

4 This is flat and round.

5 This travels through snow easily.

6 There are many of these between Mars and Jupiter.

8 This goes around Earth.

10 A very nice smell

11 This is the answer to 8 x 10.

Down ↓

1 Any large object in space

2 This person studies planets and stars.

3 You look through this.

6 Someone who thinks they are better than other people

7 The center of something

9 Special

telescope	unique	arrogant	eighty
asteroids	fragrance	moon	core
astronomer	body	disk	sleigh

B Complete the sentences with the words in the box.

if	will	solar system	space probes

________ (1) will continue to give us information about Mars. ________ (2) scientists build a fast spacecraft, astronauts ________ (3) travel to Mars, too. In fact, they will travel through the whole ________ (4).

matter	inner	observatory	diameter	outer

Is Saturn a(n) ________ (5) planet or an outer planet? It is a(n) ________ (6) planet, which means its ________ (7) is much larger than those of the inner planets. It has rings that you can see easily from a telescope in a(n) ________ (8). Saturn is a "gas giant," so most of its ________ (9) is gas.

C Underline the incomplete sentences. Then rewrite them to make them complete.

1 The moon has a lot of craters. Thousands of craters! Asteroids and meteorites caused these craters.

____

____

2 Someday I want to travel to Mars. Or to Ganymede. I'm not sure. If I go, will you go with me?

____

D Answer the questions.

1 What interesting fact will you remember about the universe?

____

2 Would you prefer to be an astronomer or an astronaut? Why?

____

BIG QUESTION 2

How do we know what happened long ago?

Think and write.

What do you know?

What do you want to know?

Student Book pages 26–28

UNIT 3 Get Ready

Words

A Number.

1 clay	5 peasant	9 jade
2 tomb	6 treasure	10 emperor
3 uniforms	7 army	11 armor
4 archaeologist	8 soldiers	

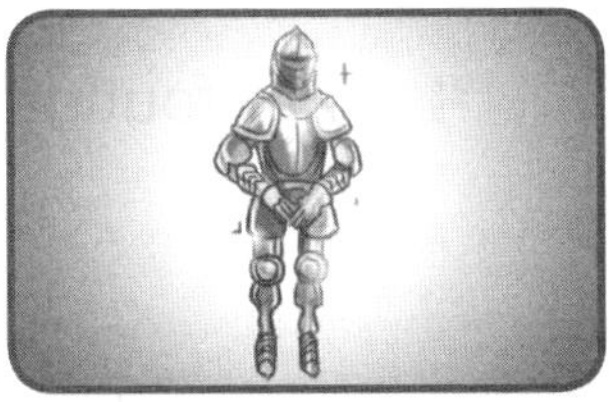

B Circle the correct words.

1 The emperor had a large **armor** / **army** / **clay** of soldiers to serve him.

2 When the emperor died, many peasants visited his **jade** / **clay** / **tomb** .

3 Recently, **treasure** / **archaeologists** / **uniforms** discovered the emperor's tomb deep underground.

4 They found **clay** / **treasure** / **armor** bowls and vases in the underground tomb.

5 Archaeologists think that soldiers in **peasant** / **jade** / **uniforms** watched over the underground emperor.

6 During that time, Chinese soldiers wore heavy **clay** / **armor** / **emperor** to protect them.

C Read. Complete the sentences with the words in the box.

jade	emperor	soldiers	peasants	treasure

Many centuries ago, a(n) ______(1)______ sat in a large room filled with beautiful ______(2)______. On his finger was a large ______(3)______ ring. However, the emperor was unhappy. Many ______(4)______ fought for the emperor and served him. He told them to bring him more treasure. They did so, but he was still unhappy. He asked a wise woman what he should do to be happy. "Give all your treasure to the poor ______(5)______ on your land," the wise woman said. The emperor gave all his treasure away, and he became a happy and joyful man.

Read

A **Read. What did archaeologists find in Germany?**

B **Read again. Think about the author's purpose. Is it to entertain, to inform, or to persuade?**

The Roman Fort of Hermeskeil

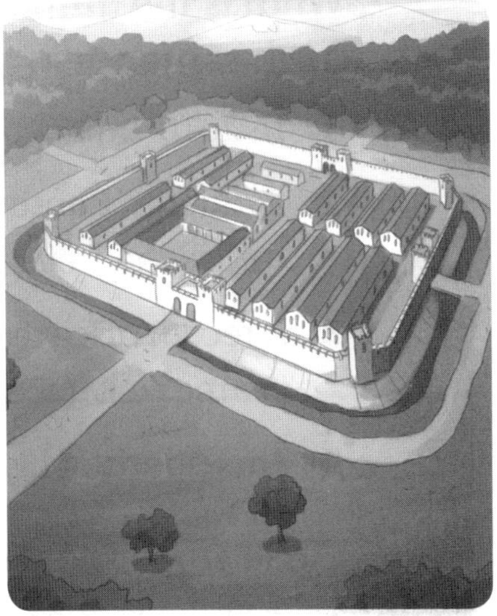

It is the year 51 BC on the border of modern France. Julius Caesar, the great Roman general, stands in front of his army. Thousands of his **soldiers** watch him carefully. There is a deep silence. Suddenly, Caesar raises his arm, and his soldiers attack the neighboring Treveri **army** with loud cries.

Think
What is the author's purpose up to now?

How do historians know this happened? A recent discovery near the German town of Hermeskeil gave them clues. In 2010, **archaeologists** believed they found a 2,000-year-old Roman fort near Hermeskeil. A fort is a place where an army can stay safely. They found parts of the fort. However, they couldn't prove it was Roman.

Then, one year later, they made an important discovery. Between two stones, they found pieces of **clay** and a nail from a Roman soldier's shoe. Shoemakers put these nails around the bottom of the shoe to keep it together. Roman soldiers walked far, and the nails kept the shoes strong. These shoes were an important part of the Roman soldier's **uniform**. The pattern on the nail proved that it was 2,000 years old.

Think
What is the author's purpose for this paragraph?

Archaeologists now know that Julius Caesar and his army were in the area at that time. They think the Roman army fought the local Treveri army and chased them away. The archaeologists hope to find more information about this interesting time in history. Today, they are still searching for clues and treasure.

Student Book page 29

Understand

Comprehension

A **What does the discovery of the 2,000-year-old Roman fort teach you? What else do you want to know about life in Germany and France 2,000 years ago?**

____

____

B **What is the author's purpose for each sentence below? Write the number of each sentence in the correct box.**

1 In 2010, archaeologists believed they found a 2,000-year-old Roman fort.

2 Suddenly, Caesar raises his arm, and his soldiers attack the Treveri army with loud cries.

3 A recent discovery near the German town of Hermeskeil gave them clues.

4 Thousands of his soldiers watch him carefully.

To Inform	To Entertain
1	

C **Circle True (T) or False (F).**

1 Archaeologists found a soldier's shoe between the stones. T F

2 The Roman fort is in modern Germany. T F

3 Archaeologists have stopped looking for clues now. T F

D **Words in Context** **Read, write, and match.**

battle ~~general~~ ancient coffin

[d] 1 Julius Caesar was a great Roman general.

[ ] 2 Archaeologists found a __________ inside the tomb.

[ ] 3 Julius Caesar sent his soldiers into __________ many times.

[ ] 4 The __________ fort is almost gone now.

a
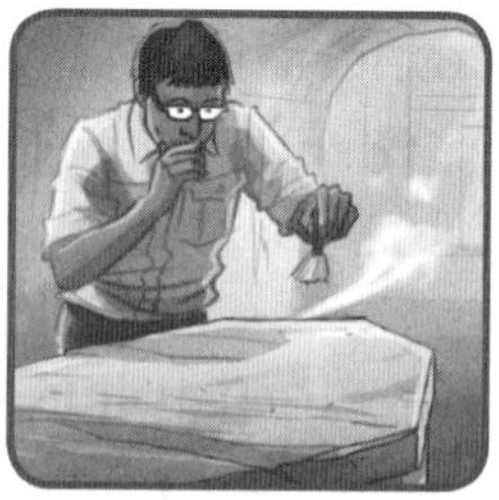

b

c

d

Student Book page 32

Grammar in Use

A Study the grammar.

Learn Verbs Followed by Infinitives

appear (to be)	hope (to meet)	plan (to study)
expect (to see)	learn (to drive)	seem (to have)

The archaeologists **hope to find** more information about this interesting time in history.

There **appear to be** / **don't appear to be** pieces of clay in the area.

He **expected to find** / **didn't expect to find** a lot of treasure in one place.

Did she **learn to label** all of the pieces correctly? Yes, she did. / No, she didn't.

What does he **plan to study** at university? He **plans to study** archaeology.

B Underline the verb before the infinitive. Then circle the infinitive.

1 Raji chose to write about the first Roman emperor for his history report.

2 The Treveri people didn't expect to see such a large Roman army.

3 Do the archaeologists plan to dig in this area much longer?

4 What time and place in history did you decide to research?

5 Gabrielle seems to be unhappy with her history test score.

6 The general didn't appear to be nervous before the battle.

7 Did Diego agree to take you to the museum?

8 What did the students learn to do at the archaeological site?

C Read. Then write the sentence with the correct infinitives.

1 The archaeologist didn't forget to labeled each of the items.

The archaeologist didn't forget to label each of the items.

2 Julius Caesar chose to attacks the Treveri army.

3 Do the archaeologists hope finding more Roman treasure?

4 What did the Roman shoemakers learn make so well?

5 The fort near Hermeskeil seems to being a real Roman fort.

D Unscramble the sentences.

1 promised / harder / He / study / to

2 find / the / She / treasure / to / expect / didn't

3 visit / you / museum / Did / plan / to / the

4 they / meet / did / Where / agree / to

E Answer the questions.

1 What historical places do you hope to visit someday?

2 Where did you first learn to speak English?

Word Study

cyclist	cartoonist	dentist	florist	tourist	pianist

A **Read and write. Circle the *-ist* suffix.**

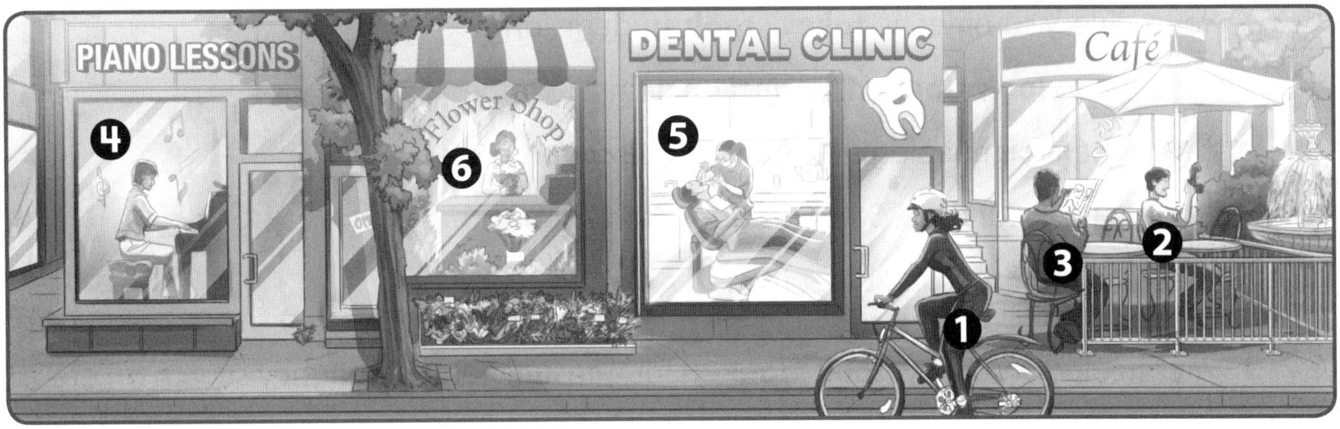

1 ______________ 2 ______________ 3 ______________

4 ______________ 5 ______________ 6 ______________

B **Complete the sentences with words from the box.**

1 Sujeong wears a white jacket in her office. She has assistants to help her. People sit in a chair and open their mouths so she can see their teeth. Sujeong is a ______________ .

2 George loves to get on airplanes and see other places. He always has his camera to take pictures. He stays at inexpensive hotels to save money. George is a ______________ .

3 Hala wears a helmet and light clothing when she does her sport. She rides many kilometers each day. Hala is a ______________ .

4 Alex works for a television show for children. He draws pictures of cute characters doing very funny things. He draws many pictures every day. Alex is a ______________ .

5 Maria practices her instrument every day. It has white and black keys. She performs for people at a concert hall every weekend. Maria is a ______________ .

6 Kenta took over his parents' business. People go to his shop on special days. His shop smells very fragrant. Kenta is a ______________ .

Writing Study

A **Circle the correct verbs.**

1 Yesterday the archaeologists **begin** / **began** their work early because the sun **is** / **was** so hot that day. They **decide** / **decided** to **stop** / **stopped** at 11:00 a.m.

2 Mr. Endo teaches history at the high school in our town. Every summer he **takes** / **took** students on a field trip to **look** / **looked** for ancient items near the river, where archaeologists **discover** / **discovered** a Roman fort years ago. Students often **find** / **found** pieces of clay pots and other items.

3 Archaeologists always **look** / **looked** for unusual items when they search an area. For example, they may **find** / **found** a stone that has a strange shape. It may be an ancient Roman stone that soldiers **use** / **used** to **make** / **made** roads.

B **Write a paragraph about something that happened long ago. Use at least one verb followed by an infinitive. Be sure that the verbs are all in the past tense.**

Julius Caesar and his soldiers **marched** all morning through the hills. By noon, they **were** only 20 kilometers from the Roman fort. The sun **was** hot, and the men **needed** food and water. After lunch, Caesar **decided to let** the men rest for one hour.

Words

A Unscramble the words.

sedimentary rock ash discover dinosaur paleontologist
examine ravine pastime skull excavate layer

1 _ _ _ _ _
k l u l s

2 _ _ _ _ _ _ _
m e a x e n i

3 _ _ _ _ _ _ _ _
v o r i d s e c

4 _ _ _ _ _ _
e a n r v i

5 _ _ _ _ _ _ _ _
a i u d r o n s

6 _ _ _ _ _
a e r l y

7 _ _ _ _ _ _ _
t a e p s i m

8 _ _ _
s a h

9 _ _ _ _ _ _ _ _
a t c a e x e v

10 _ _ _ _ _ _ _ _ _ _ _ _ _ _
t i l a p o g o e t s o n l

11 _ _ _ _ _ _ _ _ _ _ _   _ _ _ _
y e t i e d s a m r n   c r k o

B Read and number.

1 layer 2 ravine 3 ash
4 skull 5 examine 6 paleontologist

☐ a
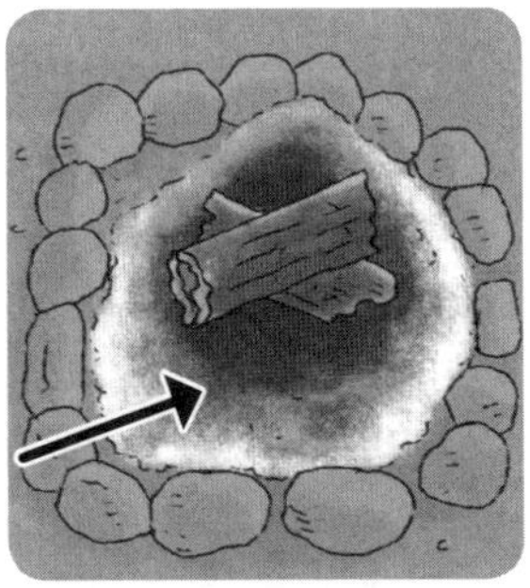

☐ b

☐ c

☐ d

☐ e

☐ f
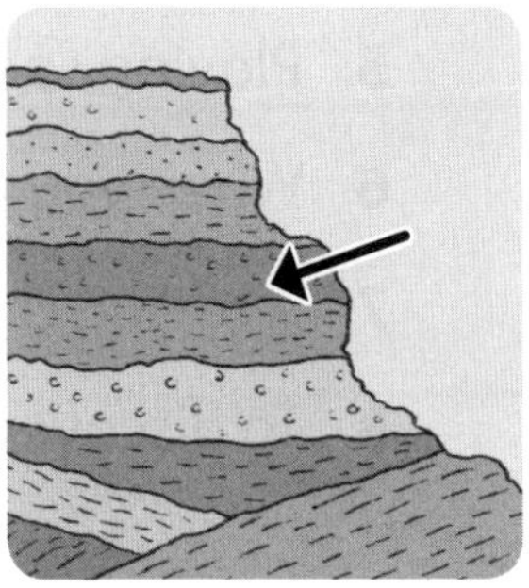

C Circle the best answers for each sentence.

1 The **ravine** / **paleontologist** discovered the dinosaur **pastime** / **skull**.

2 The paleontologists dug through the **discover** / **layers** of **sedimentary rock** / **dinosaur**.

3 Amy's favorite **pastime** / **layer** is to read about **excavate** / **dinosaurs**.

4 The students walked down into the **examine** / **ravine** to see the layer of **ash** / **discover**.

5 Frank went to the museum to **examine** / **discover** his findings from the **pastime** / **dinosaur** dig.

6 They **discovered** / **layered** a bone in the ruins that had to be **sedimentary rock** / **excavated**.

D Complete the sentences with words from the box.

dinosaur	discover	excavate	examine	paleontologists

First, ________________ (1) take shovels and ________________ (2) an area that might have ________________ (3) bones. If they are fortunate, they will ________________ (4) some bones. They will then ________________ (5) these bones to learn more about them. Finding new fossils is a lot of work!

E Circle True (T) or False (F).

1 A skull is a bone that protects the head. T F

2 Ravines may show layers of sedimentary rock. T F

3 Paleontologists only examine dinosaurs. T F

4 When something burns, it turns into ash. T F

5 Playing soccer is a pastime. T F

6 When you examine something, you take a quick look. T F

7 A ravine is a high place. T F

8 To discover something means to find something new. T F

Read

A Read. Why is the Karoo a famous place?

B Read again. As you read, make predictions.

Karen of the Karoo

Karen lived with her parents in the Karoo Basin of South Africa. The Karoo was famous for plant and animal fossils. Karen's father was a **paleontologist**, and Karen enjoyed looking at all the dinosaur bones in his office. She hoped to **discover** her own dinosaur bone someday.

Think
Do you think that Karen will find a dinosaur bone? Why or why not?

Every summer, Karen's father invited paleontologists from around the world to the Karoo. As they hiked through the dry land, he would show them fossil samples within the **layers** of **sedimentary rock** and **ash**.

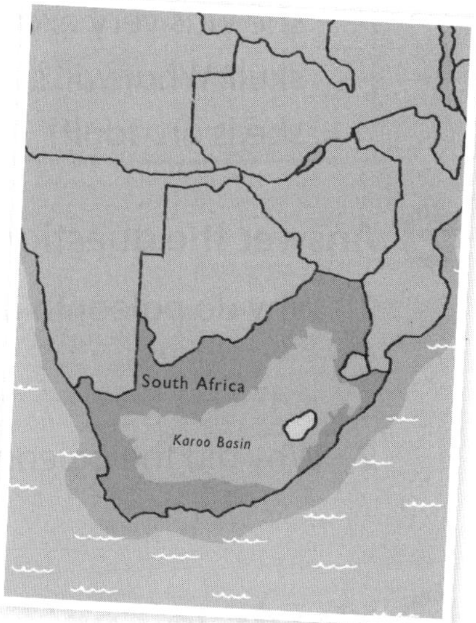

This summer, Karen asked her father if she could go along on the hike. He agreed, but he asked her to stay close by. As they drove to the trail, Karen's heart beat quickly with excitement. There were so many places to explore!

The hike was interesting, but Karen was too curious to stay on the trail. Without asking, she ran down into a nearby **ravine** and looked among the rocks. Then, she heard her father's voice calling to her. She ran up the side of the ravine. Suddenly, she spotted something white and shiny. "Dad!" she shouted excitedly.

Think
What do you think the shiny white object will be?

Karen's father stood at the top of the ravine with the other people. They looked worried until Karen pointed to the shiny object. All the paleontologists **examined** it. They nodded to each other in surprise. It was the **skull** of a dinosaur, a dinosaur nobody knew about! The paleontologists took pictures and shook Karen's hand. Her father smiled. "Karen," he said. "You are now the youngest paleontologist in the Karoo!"

Student Book page 37

Comprehension

A Think about Karen's story. Do you think it could really happen? Why or why not?

B Write a prediction based on each question.

Question	My Prediction
1 Karen found the skull of a new dinosaur in the ravine. What will paleontologists do there now?	Paleontologists will
2 Karen's father is very proud of his daughter and calls her a paleontologist. What will Karen do when her father has another group hike in the Karoo?	
3 Karen likes dinosaur bones, and she was very excited to find the skull. What will she become when she is an adult?	

C Answer the questions.

1 Why do paleontologists from around the world like to visit the Karoo?

2 Why did the paleontologists take pictures of the skull and shake Karen's hand?

D **Words in Context** Read and write.

favorite	dream	determine	tripped

1 Karen's father will try to ______ the age of the skull.

2 Jerome ______ on the rock, but fortunately he didn't fall down.

3 Abe's ______ pastime is looking at dinosaur bones.

4 Karen's ______ is to find a dinosaur skull.

Student Book page 40

Grammar in Use

A Study the grammar.

Learn Verbs Followed by Gerunds

dislike (excavating)	appreciate (learning)	recommend (resting)
imagine (discovering)	consider (going)	stop (studying)

Karen **enjoyed looking** at all the dinosaur bones in her father's office.

I **enjoyed talking** / **didn't enjoy talking** to the paleontologists after the hike.

He **didn't begin writing** / **began writing** his report on dinosaurs after dinner.

Did you **finish excavating** the area in the ravine? Yes, I did. / No, I didn't.

What does she **like doing** after her homework? She **likes watching** TV.

B Underline the verbs. Then circle the gerunds.

1 Jacob didn't start (building) his dinosaur model yet.

2 Karen likes looking at all the bones in her father's office.

3 Did Miguel finish examining the skull this morning?

4 Karen's father enjoys taking her on hikes in the Karoo.

5 Where did you practice digging before you went to the site?

C Read. Then correct the sentences.

watching

1 I enjoy ~~watch~~ films about ancient history.

2 The people in the Karoo like show visitors their area.

3 Lars stopped do research for his dinosaur report.

4 I recommend take a break before we label these items.

5 Marin considered study paleontology at university.

6 Natasha disliked get her hands dirty when she looked for bones.

Student Book page 41

D Complete the sentences with the verbs in parentheses.

My friend Ben enjoys ______________ (read) about dinosaurs a lot. He told me that he imagines ______________ (find) a dinosaur bone someday. In fact, on Saturday he looked for dinosaur bones on his grandfather's farm all day. He only stopped ______________ (dig) so that he could eat. I like ______________ (talk) to Ben about dinosaurs. He knows so much about them. I really hope he considers ______________ (study) paleontology at university when he is older.

(Blanks numbered 1–5.)

E Unscramble the sentences.

1 visiting / likes / museum / Sarah / the / science

____

2 father / enjoyed / with / Karen / hiking / her

____

3 skull / pictures / paleontologists / finished / The / taking / the / of

____

F Answer the questions.

1 What do you prefer eating for breakfast?

____

2 What do you enjoy doing as a pastime?

____

3 What did you finish doing recently?

____

Word Study

relief	grief	niece	piece	thief	brief

A Read. Circle the *ie* words with a *long e* sound. Then match.

1 My niece and her friend presented their science project about dinosaurs to the class.

2 The broken dinosaur bone caused the museum director a lot of grief.

3 The paleontologist took a brief rest under a beech tree.

4 A thief ran from the museum with a dinosaur skull that he stole.

5 The museum director gave a sigh of relief when she finally had the whole skull.

6 A piece of the skull was missing, but a little boy found it and gave it to the museum director.

a

b

c

d

e

f

B Complete the sentences with the words in the box.

My ______ (1) has a large collection of fossils that she found herself. One day she discovered that one of the fossils was gone! This caused her a lot of ______ (2). Who was the ______ (3)? During a ______ (4) search around the fossils, she found a ______ (5) of a cookie under the table. She ran to the living room and laughed with ______ (6). Her baby brother was playing with the missing fossil!

Student Book page 43

Writing Study

A **Read. Circle the correct verbs. Write *C* if the underlined word is a count noun and *NC* if it is a noncount noun.**

1 A ravine **is** / **are** a good place to see layers of sedimentary rock. C

2 Paleontologists **excavates** / **excavate** carefully for bones. ____

3 Coal **is** / **are** a kind of sedimentary rock. ____

4 This dinosaur skull **has** / **have** huge teeth. ____

5 Water **wash** / **washes** sedimentary rock into rivers and lakes. ____

6 Many children **visit** / **visits** the Karoo to see the fossils there. ____

7 Volcanic ash **help** / **helps** scientists determine the age of a bone. ____

8 My niece **go** / **goes** to South Africa every summer to study fossils. ____

B **Write a paragraph about something old that people might look for in the ground. Use at least one verb followed by a gerund. Be sure that verbs correctly match the count and noncount nouns.**

> Many people **enjoy looking** for old coins in the ground. **Coins fall** out of pockets and might stay in the ground for years. Some **people use** a special machine that makes a sound when it discovers a coin. **Dirt comes** off the coins easily when you wash them.

Wrap Up

Writing

A Read. Label the parts of the report.

A Photograph from the Past

Recently, I saw a photograph that someone took in Germany in 1890. The picture surprised me. I learned many things about the past from examining it.

The picture shows three girls walking to school on a sunny spring morning. They are dressed in cotton skirts. Two of the girls have leather book bags. This taught me that people used a lot of natural materials to make things at that time.

There is a horse and wagon in front of the girls. I learned that people used horses for transportation then. I can imagine the sound of the horse's hooves on the street.

Behind the girls, there is a bakery with fresh cakes in the window. I can almost smell the cakes and fresh bread. This taught me that people went shopping and ate delicious food, just as we do.

This photograph taught me that life was simpler in those days. People used animals for transportation, and they also used natural materials to make things. However, children still needed to eat and go to school, just as we do today.

B Plan your descriptive report. Choose a photograph. Then organize your ideas.

My Photograph: Time ________		**Place** ________		
I see ________	I hear ________	I smell ________	I taste ________	I touch ________
I learned ________				

C Now go to your notebook to write your own descriptive report about an old photograph. Then read and revise it.

My writing checklist:

- ☐ I included an interesting title.
- ☐ I introduced the photograph in the introduction paragraph.
- ☐ In the body, I described what I saw, heard, smelled, tasted, and touched.
- ☐ In the body, I wrote what I learned from the photograph.
- ☐ I summarized what I learned in the conclusion paragraph.

What did you learn?

A Read and number.

1 paleontologist
2 thief
3 archaeologist
4 tourist
5 treasure
6 emperor
7 peasant
8 soldier
9 general
10 uniforms

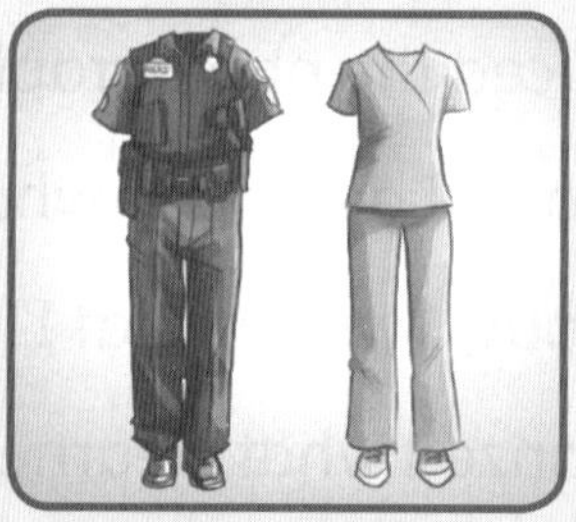

BIG QUESTION 2

How do we know what happened long ago?

B Complete the sentences with word pairs from the box.

layers–ash ~~excavate–skull~~ jade–treasures tripped–piece dentist–examined

1 Paleontologists will **excavate** this area to try to find the **skull**.

2 The ____________ ____________ the child's teeth and mouth.

3 The emperor's ____________ ring was one of the best ____________ they found.

4 They discovered the dinosaur bones between two ____________ of ____________.

5 The little boy ____________ on a ____________ of the dinosaur skull.

C Read. Circle the correct words.

1 The paleontologists agreed **to excavate / excavating** the area right away.

2 They expected **discovering / to discover** more bones near the skull.

3 The archaeologists finished **to examine / examining** the ancient tomb today.

4 Tara forgot **labeling / to label** the bone she found in the ravine.

5 The general didn't mind **letting / to let** his soldiers wash their uniforms.

6 The tourists seem **to like / liking** the dinosaur exhibit.

D Read. Circle the correct verbs.

Clay **seem / seems**[1] to last a very long time. The terra-cotta soldiers in China **is / are**[2] made of clay. They **look / looked**[3] very good even today. Archaeologists **is / are**[4] happy that this treasure **remain / remains**[5] almost the same as when the emperor saw them. Ancient armor also **stay / stays**[6] nearly the same for many years. Jade never **change / changes**[7]. We **are / were**[8] fortunate that so many ancient items **is / are**[9] still the same today.

BIG QUESTION 3

Where does our food come from?

Think and write.

What do you know?

What do you want to know?

UNIT 5 Get Ready

Words

A Read and number.

1 leopard	5 spoil	9 bark
2 butter	6 vanilla	10 wheat
3 plantation	7 sugar cane	11 ingredients
4 cinnamon	8 steamship	

☐ 

☐ 

☐ 

☐ 

☐ 

☐ 

☐ 

☐ 

☐ 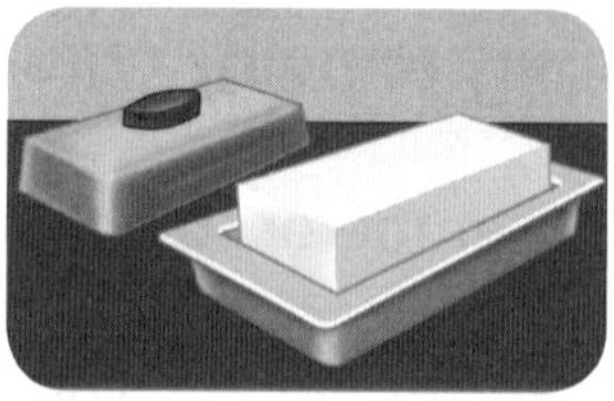

☐ 

☐ 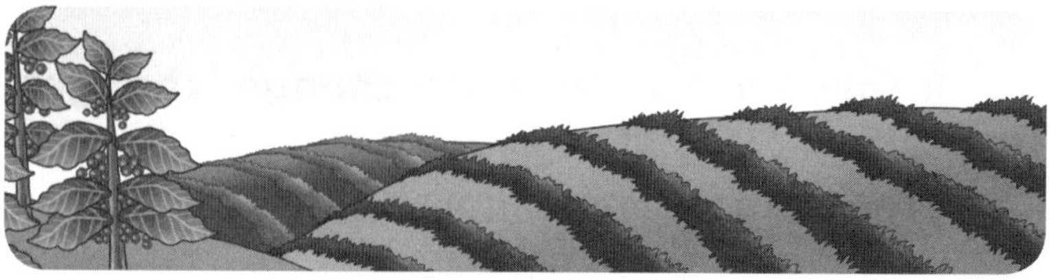

Student Book pages 46–48

B Circle the correct words.

1 **Wheat** / **Cinnamon** is a spice that people use in cooking and baking.

2 The **leopard** / **steamship** carried people from America to France.

3 Some people like the taste of **vanilla** / **ingredients** in ice cream.

4 **Leopards** / **Butter** live in Africa, India, and other countries.

5 The milk will **bark** / **spoil** if you leave it out of the fridge.

6 It takes a lot of **ingredients** / **bark** to make a chocolate cake.

7 People make **butter** / **vanilla** from cream, which comes from milk.

8 **Sugar cane** / **Bark** grows mostly in warm countries.

9 Bakers use **cinnamon** / **wheat** as the main ingredient in most breads.

10 People often grow sugar cane on large **steamships** / **plantations**.

11 The **bark** / **sugar cane** of the cinnamon tree gives us the cinnamon spice.

C Complete the paragraph with the words in the box.

ingredients	cinnamon	steamship	plantation	butter

As the ______ (1) traveled up the coast, carrying ______ (2) from a ______ (3) in Sri Lanka, a man sat on the ship eating his breakfast. On the table were some slices of bread and ______ (4). Other people sat on the deck and enjoyed the view. Inside the ship, a chef stood in his kitchen and wrote down the ______ (5) he needed to make dinner for the passengers.

Read

A **Read. What are some ingredients Pierre needs to make cookies?**

B **Read again. As you read, draw conclusions about parts of the story.**

The Greatest Dessert

Pierre was a baker who made delicious cookies in Lyon, France. His great wish was to send his daughter, Audrey, to the best baking school in Lyon, but it was too expensive.

Think

Draw a conclusion. How does Pierre feel about his daughter Audrey?

One afternoon, Pierre received a letter from the Lyon Baking Academy. "Win the Lyon Dessert Contest!" it said. "You or a family member can study for free at the Academy for one year."

Pierre was excited. Could his cookies win the contest? He phoned his friend Dion for help.

"Don't worry," Dion said. "I will talk to our friends."

Three days went by, and Pierre felt worried. Suddenly, his friends walked in carrying large packages.

"Your cookies will win, Pierre!" said Dion. "You just need the best **ingredients**. Here's the tastiest **cinnamon** from Sri Lanka."

"Here's the freshest **butter** from Holland," said Marie.

"I have flour from the finest Canadian **wheat**," said Michel.

"This sugar comes from the best Brazilian **sugar cane**," said Juliana.

"Here's delicious **vanilla** from Madagascar," said Lydia.

Pierre then saw Audrey with a large jar.

"Here is your secret ingredient, Papa," she said. "French applesauce!"

Pierre mixed the ingredients. He rolled the mixture into balls and put them in the oven. Fifteen minutes later, the cookies were ready to eat.

Think

Draw a conclusion. Why did it take three days for Pierre's friends to arrive?

"Delicious!" shouted his friends.

On Saturday, Pierre's cookies received the winning prize at the Academy. Audrey was able to study there for one year!

Today, Audrey and Pierre have the most famous bakery in Lyon. They are opening a new bakery soon. Pierre says it is all because of his friends.

Student Book page 49

Understand

Comprehension

A **What makes this story interesting? Write about two events in the story that make it interesting.**

____

____

B **Answer the questions.**

1 The baking school in Lyon was too expensive for Pierre. What conclusion can you draw from this?

____

2 Pierre used the ingredients his friends brought, and his cookies were even more delicious. What conclusion can you draw from this?

____

3 Pierre and Audrey now have a famous bakery and will open a new one soon. What conclusion can you draw from this?

____

C **Circle True (T) or False (F).**

1	Everyone in the dessert contest had to bake cookies.	T	F
2	Each of Pierre's friends brought one ingredient to him.	T	F
3	Pierre's friends thought that his cookies tasted very good.	T	F
4	Pierre and Audrey have the most famous bakery in France.	T	F

D **Words in Context** **Read and write. Change the tenses if necessary.**

gather	introduce	peel	coax

1 Before you can eat an orange, you must ______________ off the skin.

2 Audrey was happy to study baking. Her father didn't have to ______________ her.

3 Pierre's friends ______________ together yesterday to buy more ingredients.

4 Audrey ______________ herself to the teachers at the Academy last week.

Student Book page 52

Grammar in Use

A Study the grammar.

Learn **Present Continuous for Future Plans**

They	**are opening** / **aren't opening**	a new bakery soon.
She	**is taking** / **isn't taking**	a cooking class tomorrow.
I	**am buying** / **am not buying**	new ingredients on Saturday to make cookies.
Are you **planting** a garden this spring?	Yes, I am. / No, I'm not.	
What **is** he **baking** for his friends tomorrow?	He'**s baking** a cake.	

B Underline the present continuous verbs. Then circle the future time words.

1 Grace is baking a chocolate cake tomorrow for her mother's birthday.

2 The steamship is bringing sugar cane to Shanghai tomorrow afternoon.

3 Are you putting fresh cinnamon on the cookies soon?

4 I'm not making spaghetti tonight because I don't have any pasta.

5 Where is Sophie buying the fruit for the party on Friday?

6 They aren't baking cookies after dinner because they're too busy.

7 Is he driving to the supermarket at 3:00 p.m. to get the ingredients?

8 Why are you making peach pie without fresh peaches this weekend?

9 Jack isn't going to cooking school next fall because it's too expensive.

10 Who is eating vanilla ice cream with apple pie after dinner?

C Circle the correct verbs.

1 They (is / **are**) (**shopping** / buying) for fresh vegetables at the market tomorrow.

2 He (isn't / wasn't) (eating / planting) onions in his garden next summer.

3 (Were / Are) you (baking / working) fresh bread tomorrow morning?

4 What plantation (are / were) they (cooking / visiting) next Saturday?

D Read and write. Use the present continuous tense.

pick	plant	~~take~~	give

1 I __am taking__ cooking classes at the Academy next fall.

2 My uncle ________________ wheat in May. It will grow all summer.

3 The students ________________ strawberries at the farm next week.

4 The baker in our town ________________ free donuts to people tomorrow.

E Rewrite the sentences. Use the present continuous tense.

1 Chris will work on a sugar cane plantation next fall.

__Chris is working on a sugar cane plantation next fall.__

2 Will Natalie take three cooking classes next spring?

____

____

3 Mrs. Miller won't plant potatoes in her garden next April.

____

____

4 I will buy eggs next spring from my aunt, who has chickens.

____

____

Communicate

Word Study

drop off	drop by	drop back	drop out

A Read. Complete the phrasal verb in each sentence. Then number.

1 Jane dropped ____________ of the cooking contest when she got sick.

2 The farmer near our town often drops ____________ to sell his fresh eggs.

3 The truck driver dropped ____________ the bananas at the supermarket.

4 Stefan started at the front of the hike, but then he dropped ____________ .

B Complete the sentences with words from the box. Use the correct tense.

My cousin ____________ (1) our house this morning to say he was ____________ (2) of cooking school. He said he used to be the top student in his class, but then he ____________ (3) to the bottom after he got sick for two weeks. He stopped by to ____________ (4) my mom's cookbook that he was using. We all felt very bad about his decision.

Writing Study

A **Read. Circle the most interesting adjectives.**

Last week our class visited a **big** / **vast** [1] sugar cane plantation. First, we walked two hours through the **towering** / **tall** [2] stalks of sugar cane. We were **very tired** / **exhausted** [3] by the end of the hike. Next, it was time for a **good** / **delicious** [4] lunch. The chef at the plantation brought each of us a **steaming** / **hot** [5] plate of spaghetti. For dessert, we had **big** / **juicy** [6] strawberries and a glass of **cold** / **icy** [7] lemonade sweetened with sugar from the plantation!

B **Write a paragraph about a delicious meal you had. Write at least one sentence with a present continuous verb to show a future plan. Be sure to use interesting adjectives.**

For my birthday, my mother made me an **elegant** lunch. She served **mouth-watering** vegetables, a **crisp** salad, and **delicate** sandwiches cut into **interesting** shapes. For dessert, I ate **creamy** vanilla ice cream with cinnamon on top. **I'm making** the same meal for my mother on her birthday next month.

UNIT 6 Get Ready

Words

local	chemical	export	convenient	package	agriculture
farmer's market	century	decrease	process	corporate farm	

A **Unscramble the words. Then solve the secret message.**

teinovnecn ___ ___(14) ___ ___ ___ ___ ___ ___ ___ ___(10)

ropxet ___(5) ___ ___ ___ ___ ___

rorcetpoa rfma ___ ___ ___ ___ ___ ___ ___ ___ ___(7)   ___(12) ___ ___ ___

lcaol ___(9) ___ ___ ___ ___(2)

cosrspe ___ ___ ___(13) ___ ___ ___ ___

kagcape ___ ___ ___ ___(4) ___ ___ ___

rergutcuila ___ ___ ___ ___(1) ___ ___ ___ ___ ___ ___ ___

rdeacsee ___(15) ___ ___ ___ ___ ___ ___ ___

cyunert ___ ___ ___ ___ ___ ___ ___(11)

rarfem's tekram ___ ___ ___ ___ ___ ___ ' ___   ___ ___(8) ___ ___ ___ ___

cacmehli ___ ___(6) ___ ___ ___(3) ___ ___ ___

Secret Message

___(1)   ___(2) ___(3) ___(4) ___(5)   ___(6) ___(7) ___(8) ___(9) ___(10) ___(6) ___(11)

___(12) ___(13) ___(14) ___(15) .

B Look and write.

chemical	corporate farm	farmer's market	century

1 
______

2 

______

3 
______

4 
______

C Match.

1 This action puts food into containers such as bottles or boxes. •
2 This action turns oranges into orange juice. •
3 Something that causes no trouble; easy to do •
4 Something in your area or neighborhood •
5 When you do this, you make something smaller or less. •
6 This gives us the food we need to live. •
7 This action sends things out of a country. •

• **a** convenient
• **b** agriculture
• **c** local
• **d** decrease
• **e** package
• **f** export
• **g** process

D Complete the sentences with the word pairs in the box.

agriculture–corporate farms	farmer's market–local
package–decrease	century–chemicals

1 A ______ usually sells fresh food from the ______ area.
2 Modern ______ includes family farms and ______ .
3 In the last ______ , people used more ______ to grow food.
4 When people ______ less food, we ______ the use of energy.

A **Read. Why is olive oil popular?**

____

____

B **Read again. As you read, try to summarize the main details and ideas of the article.**

Olive Oil: From the Tree to Your Table

Did you know that farmers grew the first olive trees over 6,000 years ago? Olive trees produce delicious olive fruit, which many people eat. However, olive growers use most olives to make olive oil.

Think
Summarize what you just read in one or two sentences.

Olive oil is very popular around the world. People use olive oil for cooking, and they eat it with food such as breads and salads. People in Greece use the most olive oil, but Italians and Spaniards use a lot, too.

This delicious oil originally comes from countries around the Mediterranean Sea. Today, Spain, Italy, and Greece produce 75 percent of the world's olive oil. Farmers in these countries grow many of the olives needed for the olive oil on small farms.

How do people **process** olives into olive oil? First, they grind the olives into a mixture. Then, they stir the mixture. This helps the oil to come together. Finally, they press the mixture to remove the oil. Some people still process olive oil by hand, but now machines do it more often. After people remove the oil, they **package** it and **export** it to countries around the world. They use ships, trains, and trucks to get the oil to the shops that sell it.

Think
Summarize the paragraph above in one or two sentences.

There are many kinds of olive oil, but extra-virgin olive oil is really delicious. It's also healthy. Would you like to taste some? Thanks to modern **agriculture**, olive oil is now **convenient** to buy. Go to your **local** supermarket and try some today!

Student Book page 57

Comprehension

A How does this reading change the way you think about how we grow food?

____

____

B Summarize each of the following topics in one or two sentences.

Who produces olive oil?	How is it processed?

C Answer the questions.

1 How do people use olive oil?

____

2 How do people process olive oil differently now?

____

3 Why do you think that machines are processing more olive oil now?

____

D **Words in Context** Read and write.

grocery store food labels organic food whole food

1 Jen doesn't like food sprayed with chemicals, so she eats

______________ .

2 Leyla goes to the ______________ twice a week to buy food.

3 It is difficult for Roberto's grandmother to read

______________ because the words are so small.

4 Andrew likes to buy ______________ from the farmer because it isn't processed.

Student Book page 60

Grammar in Use

A Study the grammar.

Learn Polite Offers

Offering an Action	Offering a Thing
Would you like to taste some olive oil? Yes, I'd like to try some.	**Would you like** some olive oil? No, thank you.
Would you like to eat an orange? Yes, I'd like that.	**Would you like** an orange? No, thanks. I wouldn't like one.

B **Read each sentence. If an action is offered, underline the verb. If a thing is offered, circle what it is.**

1 Would you like to see where they grow olives in Italy?
2 Would you like a little olive oil on your salad?
3 Would you like to make fresh lemonade with these lemons?
4 Would you like a cup of tea with your cake?
5 Would you like two cookies with your milk?
6 Would you like to buy some organic peaches at the farmer's market?
7 Would you like to plant tomatoes with me this afternoon?
8 Would you like some strawberries from Spain?
9 Would you like to read this book about organic food?
10 Would you like some delicious chocolate from Belgium?
11 Would you like to package these green beans with me?
12 Would you like to go to the grocery store with me?

C Complete the sentences with *to* or *a*.

1 Would you like ______ read my report about chemicals in food?

2 I'd like ______ juicy pineapple from Costa Rica.

3 I wouldn't like ______ bowl of rice with my steamed vegetables.

4 Would you like ______ help me bake some bread with this flour?

5 Would you like ______ kilogram of tomatoes from Mexico?

6 I wouldn't like ______ have Italian pasta for dinner.

D Unscramble the sentences.

1 kiwifruit / like / some / you / today / to / Would / pick

____

2 beef / I / a / would / kilogram / like / of / buy / to

____

3 salad / like / your / Would / pepper / you / on / some

____

E Write a polite offer.

1 You think your friend might like an orange.

Would you like an orange?

2 You think your friend might like to try some kimchi from Korea.

____

3 You think your friend might like some cheese from Holland.

____

4 You think your friend might like to work on a farm with you.

____

Student Book page 61

Communicate

Word Study

photographer	geography	dictionary	introduction	environment	conversation

A **Read each sentence. Circle the word that has four syllables. Then match.**

1 In geography class I learned that people grow rice in warmer, wetter countries.

2 The introduction in the cookbook explains why the author chose recipes from the Mediterranean.

3 My dictionary says that a tomato is a fruit that originally comes from Peru.

4 The photographer took many pictures of the olive groves in Spain, Italy, and Greece.

5 I had a nice conversation with the manager of the organic food store.

6 If people use too many chemicals to grow food, it may be bad for the environment.

a

b

c

d

e

f

B **Complete the sentences with the words in the box.**

I want to be a food ____________ (1) and travel around the world. I will take pictures and have interesting ____________ (2) with farmers, bakers, and chefs. Then I will write a book about the ____________ (3) of food. It will show where different foods grow. The beginning of the book will have an ____________ (4) about protecting our ____________ (5). The language of my book will be simple. Readers won't need a ____________ (6).

Writing Study

A **Complete the sentences with the prepositions of location in the box.**

on	next to	under	between	behind	near

1 The carrots are ______________ the onions and the potatoes.

2 The potatoes are ______________ the tomatoes.

3 There are flowers ______________ the vegetables.

4 The truck is ______________ the farmer.

5 The peaches are ______________ the truck.

6 Two women are ______________ the table.

B **Read. Then write a paragraph describing a vegetable or flower garden you planted in your imagination or for real. Make at least one polite offer. Be sure to use prepositional phrases of location.**

Would you like to see my beautiful garden? I planted three rows of vegetables **in the garden**. The carrots are **between the green beans and the spinach**. I also planted potatoes and tomatoes **behind those three rows**. Finally, I planted colorful flowers **around the garden**.

Wrap Up

Writing

A Read. Label the parts of the report.

International Hungarian Goulash

I live in Hungary, and my grandma makes the best goulash in the world! I watched her cook it yesterday, and I discovered where all the ingredients come from.

I first looked at the labels of the food that she bought at the supermarket. The tomatoes that she used came from Turkey, and the beef broth came from France.

Next, I asked Grandma where she got her fresh ingredients. The onions and peppers came from the local farmer's market, and the beef came from a local organic farm.

Finally, I searched on the Internet to get information about paprika, my favorite ingredient in Grandma's goulash. I discovered that Hungary is the home of this delicious spice. My country makes a lot of the paprika that people use around the world. The word "paprika" actually means "pepper," and there are many varieties.

Although goulash comes from Hungary, you can find the ingredients to make it wherever you live. I hope you can try this delicious dish soon!

B Plan your research report. Choose your favorite dish or a meal that you enjoy eating. Do research to find where the ingredients come from.

My Favorite Dish or Meal	
The dish or meal	
Ingredients	
Information from food labels	
Information from people	
Information from books or the Internet	

C Now go to your notebook to write your own research report about the ingredients for your dish or meal and where they come from.

My writing checklist:

- ☐ I introduced the dish or meal in the introduction paragraph.
- ☐ I explained where I did research and what I learned in the main paragraphs.
- ☐ I summarized what I learned in the conclusion paragraph.

Student Book page 64

What did you learn?

BIG QUESTION 3

Where does our food come from?

Review

A **Write the words.**

leopard wheat food label butter photographer
chemicals farmer's market cinnamon
steamship grocery store vanilla conversation

1 ______________________ 7 ______________________

2 ______________________ 8 ______________________

3 ______________________ 9 ______________________

4 ______________________ 10 ______________________

5 ______________________ 11 ______________________

6 ______________________ 12 ______________________

B Circle the correct words.

On my visit to an organic farm, the farmer, Mr. Gaffney, **peeled / introduced** (1) me to the science of chemical-free **agriculture / bark** (2). His way of farming is not **local / convenient** (3). In fact, it takes a lot of work. However, Mr. Gaffney believes in organic food, and he wants to **export / process** (4) it to other countries someday.

C Complete the sentences with the words in the box. Circle the future time word.

environment	~~dropping off~~	ingredients	geography
package	organic food	drop by	gathering

1 We're **dropping off** some organic apples at the farmer's market this afternoon.

I'd like to try one before you __________ them in those boxes.

2 Some of the students are __________ tomorrow morning to bake a cake for our teacher.

I'd like to bring some __________ .

3 Our family isn't using chemicals in our garden next summer to help the __________ .

Would you like to grow __________ with us?

4 I'm studying for a __________ test tonight.

Would you like to __________ my house and study with me?

D Read. Replace the underlined adjectives with more interesting ones. Circle the prepositional phrases of location.

beautiful

It is a <u>pretty</u> morning. I reach behind my bed and get my <u>old</u> work clothes. It's time for me to do some gardening. I eat a <u>nice</u> breakfast and walk outside. The sunlight is <u>warm</u>. I see that there are some <u>bad</u> weeds near the carrots. My shovel is next to the garden, so I pick it up and dig out the weeds. The flowers look <u>dry</u>, so I water them. Then, I rest under a tree because I'm <u>tired</u>. I don't mind working. Gardening is <u>fun</u>!

BIG QUESTION 4

Why do we make art?

Think and write.

What do you know?

____

____

____

____

____

____

____

____

____

What do you want to know?

____

____

____

____

____

____

____

____

____

Student Book pages 66–68

UNIT 7 Get Ready

Words

prodigy three-dimensional paintbrushes
string carpenter pastels street painter
sketch shapes canvas sculptor

A Look and write.

1 
____

2 
____

3 
____

4 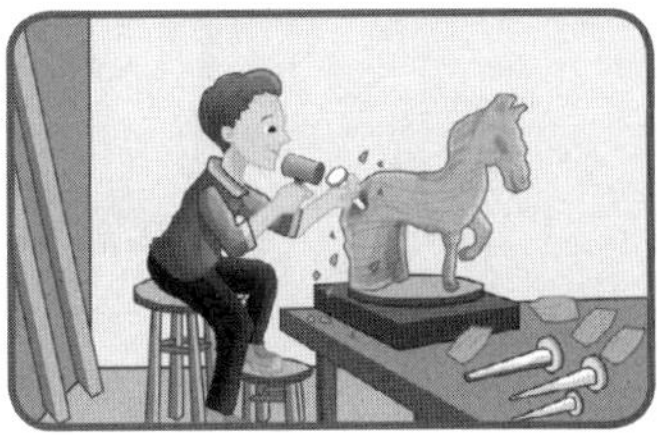
____

B Look and write the words.

1 ______________________

2 ______________________

3 ______________________

4 ______________________

5 ______________________

6 ______________________

7 ______________________

C Match. Then number.

1 The painting of the new museum is good, but it looks a little flat.

2 Oil paints are too difficult for children to use when they paint.

3 Leonardo da Vinci painted many masterpieces during his lifetime.

4 Many modern artists use a variety of interesting materials in their art.

5 In art class, the students are studying ovals, triangles, squares, and circles.

a However, many of his great works started out as sketches.

b These include paper and string.

c They are learning how to use these shapes to make realistic sketches.

d I want it to look more three-dimensional.

e Pastels are much easier for them to use.

D Complete the sentences with the words in the box.

paintbrushes	canvas	prodigy	carpenter	street painter	sculptor

1 William is a ________________. He paints with large ________________ so that everyone walking through the city can enjoy his work.

2 Christine is quite a ________________. She is only seven years old, but she can already make realistic animals out of clay. She says she wants to be a famous ________________ when she grows up.

3 Roger is a ________________, but he also likes to paint. During his lunch break, he stops working with wood and paints on a ________________ that he keeps in his truck.

Student Book page 68

A Read. Why do you think these two artists create art?

____

____

B Read again. As you read, remember to look at the text features. These will help you to understand more about the reading.

Creating Art from Life

Art from Trash

Linda Wise is the manager of a garbage company in California, so she sees how many things people throw away. Linda says, "Objects seem to lose their usefulness so quickly in our society. But many things are still useful."

Linda Wise
"I don't see waste. I see potential."

To show this, Linda started to turn people's trash into beautiful **three-dimensional** works of art. It seems that she can make art out of anything. As a **sculptor**, her art receives many awards. The city of Fortuna, California, has three of her sculptures on display. People in the city like seeing art in their town. Many children want to be artists like Ms. Wise.

Robert Aswani
Thursday Market Day

Painting African Life

Robert Aswani was born in 1971 in the African country of Kenya. He taught himself to draw and paint as a young boy. His teachers felt he was a **prodigy**. They often asked him to draw **sketches** on the blackboard. Robert always painted colorful paintings after he visited the African markets with his mother. "The marketplace is full of life and color," he says. Today, Robert uses his **paintbrushes** and **canvas** to show the beautiful scenes of Africa. These scenes include sunrises, sunsets, markets, and the life of the Maasai people of Kenya. People from around the world buy his paintings.

Robert Aswani
"Painting is something I have loved since I was young."

Think
How do the text features help you understand the artists?

Comprehension

A Which artist's work do you like and why?

____

____

B Match a text feature to an example from the reading. Then match the example to its meaning.

Text Feature	Example	Meaning
1 Title	a Art from Trash	f Artists get their ideas from the world around them.
2 First heading	b "I don't see waste."	g This artist paints the beauty of the surrounding culture.
3 Second heading	c *Thursday Market Day*	h This person says that everything is useful.
4 Visual	d Creating Art from Life	i This artist makes art from things other people don't want.
5 Caption	e Painting African Life	j This painting shows a scene of African women shopping.

C Answer the questions.

1 What does Linda Wise show through her art?

____

2 What does Robert Aswani show through his art?

____

D **Words in Context** Read and write.

complex	washable	combines	fascination

1 I have a ______________ with African paintings.

2 Linda Wise ______________ trash with art.

3 The artist's sketch is very ______________ .

4 Kindergarten classrooms use ______________ paint.

Student Book page 72

Grammar in Use

A Study the grammar.

Learn **Indefinite Pronouns**

Person	Thing
Someone in Europe bought one of Aswani's paintings.	Do you need **something** from the art supply store?
Does **anyone** here know who painted the *Mona Lisa*?	She can make art out of **anything**.
Everyone was quiet in the art museum.	Did he make **everything** in this room?

B Circle the correct indefinite pronoun.

1 I saw a beautiful painting of a young girl in Peru. **Someone** / **Anyone** was standing beside her.

2 **Everyone** / **Anyone** likes your sketch. They think the different shapes are really nice.

3 I think **someone** / **anyone** can paint. For example, children are great artists!

4 Our teacher puts **something** / **everything** we paint on display in the classroom.

C Match. Then complete the sentences with the words in the box.

someone	anything	something	~~anyone~~

1 I need to make a painting of a person. It can be a man or a woman. It can be a child or an adult.

2 I like to paint many things. I see beauty in nature, in cities, and everywhere I look.

3 I want to paint a person who looks young and strong. I'm looking for a person who has a lot of energy.

4 I want to paint a scene that is filled with color and energy. I want people to look at my painting and say, "Wow!"

a I want to paint ______ who is good at sports.

b I will paint **anyone**.

c I'm really happy to paint ______.

d I want to paint ______ really special.

D Write the missing half of each indefinite pronoun in each sentence.

1 Is every______ in the art room now? The playground is empty.

2 ______one can enjoy looking at art on the Internet. There are many good websites.

3 Did you buy every______ we need for the art supply cupboard?

4 There is some______ very special about the paintings of Vincent van Gogh.

E Unscramble the sentences.

1 everyone / paintbrush / Does / a / have

______

______

2 wood / can / Sculptors / anything / from / make

______

______

3 museum / I / something / from / art / bought / the

______

______

4 painting / park / Is / in / anyone / the

______

______

F Rewrite the sentences with the correct indefinite pronouns.

1 There is anything I would like you to do.

______

2 Something used for this work of art comes from trash.

______

3 I met everyone yesterday who is a street painter.

______

4 Someone can go to the city art museum. It's free of charge.

______

Word Study

A Match. Then write the words. Write the verbs in the correct tense.

dissatisfied	disorganized	dishonest	~~disprove~~	disability	distrust

1 dis + prove
2 dis + organized
3 dis + trust
4 dis + satisfied
5 dis + ability
6 dis + honest

a The art teacher was very unhappy with his students because the art room was so messy and ________________.

b The tourists were ________________ with the museum tour because some of the exhibitions weren't open to the public.

c Many famous artists painted beautiful works of art even though they had a ________________, such as poor eyesight.

d Jack thought Michelangelo painted the *Mona Lisa*, but I **disproved** it by showing him the painting in a book about Leonardo da Vinci.

e The ________________ artist said that he painted the landscape, but actually his wife painted it.

f The art dealer said that all of the sculptures he sold were from ancient Rome, but Paul ________________ him.

B Complete the paragraph with the words in the box.

prove	honest	disorganized	dissatisfied	trust	ability

I really enjoy painting in art class, but I'm ________________ (1) with my paintings. I don't think I have a great ________________ (2). Also, my oil paints are very ________________ (3), so I often can't find the right color. I was ________________ (4) with my teacher and told her I wasn't a good artist. She said that she was a good teacher, however, and that I should ________________ (5) her teaching ability. I'm going to work harder and ________________ (6) that she is right!

Student Book page 75

Writing Study

A **Rewrite each pair of sentences to make them one sentence with a compound predicate.**

1 As the sun rose, the artist went outside with his easel. He began to paint.

As the sun rose, the artist went outside with his easel and began to paint.

2 Ashley drew a sketch of her house. She gave it to her father for his birthday.

3 The street painter finished his painting. He then stepped onto it.

4 My father builds houses on weekdays. He makes sculptures on weekends.

5 The young prodigy won a painting competition. She received a cash prize.

B **Read. Then write a paragraph about a work of art you or someone else made. Use at least one sentence with an indefinite pronoun. Be sure to use sentences with compound predicates.**

I made **something** for my mother in art class. First, I **took a piece of modeling clay and rolled it into five balls**. Then, I sculpted the balls into different shapes. Finally, I **painted the shapes and attached them to a piece of red cardboard**. It's unusual but beautiful!

Words

A Find and circle.

c	o	t	l	b	s	h	a	d	i	n	g
p	f	e	g	r	w	m	s	u	c	y	h
e	e	x	h	i	b	i	t	i	o	n	g
r	d	t	x	l	e	n	p	v	n	b	e
s	a	u	f	l	e	l	a	p	t	v	b
p	s	r	t	i	m	w	e	h	r	s	x
e	c	e	l	a	n	d	s	c	a	p	e
c	r	o	d	n	h	n	t	g	s	b	o
t	o	t	i	t	x	m	d	f	t	i	j
i	l	q	n	k	q	z	e	m	a	r	f
v	r	k	s	t	a	i	n	e	d	i	t
e	g	o	h	l	e	c	a	p	s	w	m

texture
brilliant
stained
pale
frame
contrast
exhibition
perspective
landscape
space
shading

B Match.

1 shading ______

2 frame ______

3 exhibition ______

4 contrast ______

5 landscape ______

6 perspective ______

7 brilliant ______

8 stained ______

9 space ______

a

b

c

d

e

f

g

h

i
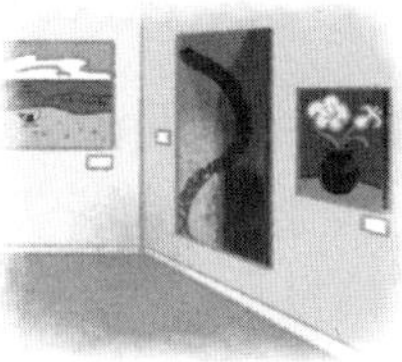

Student Book page 76

C Circle the correct words.

1 The artist used bright colors to paint the **pale** / **brilliant** sunset.

2 I can understand why Jose paints **landscapes** / **frames**. He likes to be outdoors.

3 The joggers in Amy's painting are all the same size. There is no **texture** / **perspective**.

4 This Friday, I'm going to see a(n) **contrast** / **exhibition** of modern art at the museum.

5 The **shading** / **space** of the woman's face in the sketch is very good.

6 Unfortunately, my painter's apron is badly **pale** / **stained**.

D Complete the sentences with words from the box.

frames	exhibition	space	landscape	texture	perspective	pale	contrast

1 Oil paint can be very thick. It can give a painting a lot of ________________ .

2 The desert sky in the painting looks ________________ , but the mountains are colorful.

3 I really don't like the large, fancy ________________ around some old paintings.

4 You really notice small things when a painting has a lot of ________________ in it.

5 The artist painted a bright yellow moon in a black sky to show ________________ .

6 The ________________ in this painting makes the mountains seem far away.

7 The Louvre had a(n) ________________ of Picasso's art when the artist was 90.

8 The view from Maria's bedroom window was like a(n) ________________ painting.

E Circle True (T) or False (F).

1 You can sometimes see sculptures at an exhibition. T F

2 Frames are usually very colorful. T F

3 Pale colors have a strong contrast with each other. T F

4 An artist's fingers can be stained with paint. T F

5 The stars are more brilliant on a dark night. T F

6 Landscape paintings always have people in them. T F

Read

A **Read. Why does Tam want to paint a picture of her grandmother?**

B **Read. As you read, remember to stop and make value judgments.**

Grandma's Beauty

Tam loved to paint. As a nine-year-old girl in the Vietnamese city of Can Tho, she found many places and faces to paint. She painted **landscapes** along the river. She painted rice farmers and floating market sellers. However, there was one face she wanted to paint more than any other.

"Grandma," she offered again at dinner. "Shall I paint a picture of you?"

Tam's grandmother was seventy years old. She laughed. "Why do you want to paint a simple old woman like me?" she asked.

"Please, Grandma," said Tam. "I'll paint your picture in the park early tomorrow morning. The air will be cool."

Tam's grandmother finally agreed. The next morning she sat on a bench under two lovely plumeria trees with **brilliant** red and **pale** pink flowers.

Think
What value judgment can you make about Tam?

Tam set up her canvas and began to paint as her grandmother enjoyed the morning air. Suddenly, an old man walked by the easel. He noticed the artistic **perspective** Tam used in her painting. Another person stopped by. Soon, almost fifty people were watching Tam paint.

"I'm finished," Tam finally announced.

She showed the painting to her grandmother. The woman in the painting glowed with beauty. The **contrast** of red and pink flowers with her silver hair was lovely. The **shading** on her face made her look wise and gentle.

"Who is this?" her grandmother asked in surprise.

"It's you, Grandma," said Tam, "on the outside *and* on the inside."

The people in the park agreed that Tam was truly a great artist.

Think
What value judgment can you make about Tam's grandmother?

Student Book page 77

Understand

Comprehension

A What do you think about Tam? Are you similar to her? Why or why not? Write.

____

____

B Write the following value judgments on the chart under the correct name. Then write your own value judgment for each person.

~~She enjoys what she does.~~ She is shy about who she is.
She loves to sit and enjoy nature. She sees beauty in others.

Tam	Tam's Grandmother
She enjoys what she does.	

C Answer the questions.

1 Why does Tam paint so many places and faces in her city?

____

2 Why doesn't Tam's grandmother want Tam to paint her picture at first?

____

3 How does Tam's painting show her grandmother on the *inside*?

____

D **Words in Context** Read and write.

ignore worry famous speechless

1 Tam's grandmother was almost __________ when she saw Tam's painting.

2 Tam tried to __________ the noise in the park so she could focus on painting.

3 It is possible that Tam will become a(n) __________ artist someday.

4 Tam didn't want her grandmother to __________ about the painting.

Grammar in Use

A Study the grammar.

Learn Offers with *Shall* and *Will*

Offers with a Question	Offers with a Statement
Tim: I broke my pencil. **Paul: Shall** I **get** you another one?	**Beth:** We are out of paint. **Kara:** I'**ll ask** the teacher for more.
Tam: Grandma, **shall** I **paint** a picture of you?	**Tam:** I'**ll paint** your picture in the park.

B Use *will (I'll)* or *shall* and the verbs in the box to complete each sentence.

draw	bring	ask	carry	wash	buy	~~take~~	paint

1 "This exhibition is interesting, but I'm getting hungry."
"I'__ll__ __take__ you to the cafeteria. We can eat something there."

2 "_________ I _________ the landscape with more brilliant colors?"
"No, I think the pale colors you are using are better."

3 "I think this frame is too dark for this painting of our family."
"I'____ _________ the store manager if she can find a lighter one."

4 "I'm happy that you're painting my picture, but I'm thirsty."
"_________ I _________ you some water from the kitchen?"

5 "Wow, this sculpture is heavy! It isn't easy walking home with it."
"I'____ _________ it for you for a while."

6 "We're at the Museum of Modern Art! This is very exciting!"
"It sure is. I'____ _________ our tickets for us."

7 "I didn't know that you drew sketches of famous buildings."
"It's my hobby. _________ I _________ a sketch of your house?"

8 "Oh, no! I spilled paint on my jacket."
"Give it to me. I'____ _________ it quickly."

Student Book page 81

C **Match each situation to a polite offer. Write *will (I'll)* or *shall* to complete the offer.**

1 Your friend is cleaning up the art room by herself.

2 Your art teacher needs more paper from the supply room.

3 You take your friend to your city art museum, and he wants to see the Monet exhibit.

4 Your friend is painting a landscape, but she is cold in the outside air.

a ______ I go and get some for you?

b ______ I bring you a jacket and a scarf?

c I ______ organize the paints and paintbrushes to help you.

d I ______ take you to see his paintings.

D **Unscramble the sentences.**

1 with / exhibition / you / I'll / to / the / go

______

2 paint / of / today / Shall / you / I / picture / a

______

3 frame / you / I'll / for / find / a

______

4 teacher / I / canvas / for / Shall / another / ask / the

______

E **Rewrite the questions as statements. Rewrite the statements as questions.**

1 Shall I meet you at the art studio at 9:00 a.m.?

I'll meet you at the art studio at 9:00 a.m.

2 I'll paint the mountains smaller to add perspective.

______

3 Shall I add shading to your sketch?

______

4 I'll bring your canvas and pastels to the art room.

______

Word Study

beautiful	drab	gifted	dreary	talented	pretty

A **Match. Circle the synonyms. Then number.**

1 Adel's art teacher says that Adel is a gifted artist for his young age.

2 Everyone at the art exhibition felt that Akiko's painting of a Japanese landscape was the most beautiful.

3 The paintings in the art gallery were quite dreary. They made me feel sad.

a These drab paintings didn't have any color and were very boring.

b Even his parents agree that he is a very talented sculptor.

c They liked the pretty cherry trees that she painted in front of Mount Fuji.

☐ 

☐ 

☐ 

B **Circle the correct words.**

The *Mona Lisa* is a **beautiful** / **gifted** (1) painting by Leonardo da Vinci. Art experts say that the name of the **drab** / **pretty** (2) woman in the painting is Lisa del Giocondo. Lisa was the wife of a rich businessman, and she lived in Florence, Italy. At that time, Leonardo was a **pretty** / **talented** (3) and well-known painter, so Lisa's husband asked Leonardo to paint a portrait of his wife. The painting shows how **gifted** / **dreary** (4) the artist was. It's not a bright and colorful painting, but it is not **talented** / **dreary** (5), either. The **drab** / **gifted** (6), pale mountains behind Lisa are an example of Leonardo's use of perspective. Today, the *Mona Lisa* is one of the most famous paintings in the world.

Student Book page 83

Writing Study

A Circle the correct articles.

a painting by Marc Chagall

1. We'd like to visit **an** / **the** art gallery when we go to London.
2. **A** / **The** shape of this sculpture is really unique.
3. Jason decided to draw **a** / **the** three-dimensional sketch of his house.
4. Many people like **an** / **the** art of Marc Chagall.
5. All you need to begin painting is **a** / **the** paintbrush and some paints.
6. This landscape painting needs **a** / **the** simple wooden frame.
7. **A** / **The** shading of the person's face in this sketch is very good.
8. The sky around the setting sun was **a** / **the** brilliant red color.
9. I like **an** / **the** empty space around the children in this painting.
10. Rachel may paint a landscape, or she may paint **a** / **an** bowl of fruit.

B Write a paragraph about a famous artist you like. Make at least one offer using *shall* or *will*. Be sure to use the correct articles *a*, *an*, and *the* in your sentences.

> **Shall I tell you about my favorite artist?** His name is Johannes Vermeer, and he was **a** very talented painter. He painted **the** famous portrait called *Girl with a Pearl Earring*. **The** model in **the** painting is **an** interesting-looking girl wearing **a** scarf and **a** pearl earring.

Wrap Up

Writing

A Read this opinion essay about the writer's favorite work of art. Label the four parts of the report.

Starry Night by Vincent van Gogh

Vincent van Gogh painted many beautiful works of art. However, I think his painting *Starry Night* is my favorite. There are three reasons why I think so.

First, in *Starry Night*, van Gogh painted swirling lines through the sky, around the moon, and around the stars. This movement helps me to see the beauty and energy of the night sky. The moon and stars are full of light, and they make me feel warm inside. Next, the little town below the stars looks very peaceful. I imagine that children can see the stars through their bedroom windows. Finally, there is a strong contrast between the dark tree in front of the scene and the bright sky. This contrast makes the sky look even more beautiful.

I am thankful to Vincent van Gogh for this beautiful work of art. The swirling sky, the beautiful stars, and the peaceful town are special to me. It will always be my favorite work of art.

B Plan your opinion essay. Choose your favorite work of art. Write three reasons why it's your favorite.

My Favorite Work of Art: ______________________

First Reason	Second Reason	Third Reason

C Now go to your notebook to write your own opinion essay about your favorite work of art.

My writing checklist:

- ☐ I introduced the work of art and wrote my opinion in the first paragraph.
- ☐ In the body, I gave three reasons why I have my opinion.
- ☐ I gave a brief summary of my reasons and an interesting final thought.

What did you learn?

BIG QUESTION 4

Why do we make art?

Review

A Complete the puzzle.

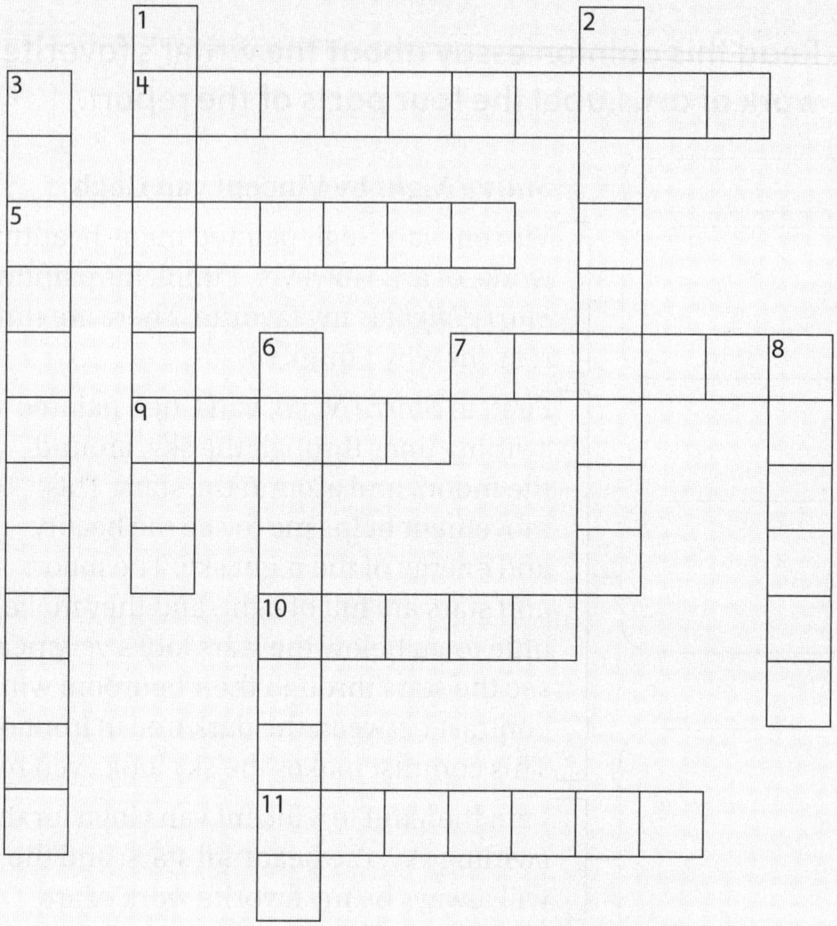

Across →

4 Artists show their art at this.

5 This artist may use wood or clay.

7 Artists paint on this.

9 This goes around a painting.

10 The empty area between things

11 A young person with great ability

Down ↓

1 Nice to look at

2 Not truthful

3 Unhappy; not pleased

6 A scene with trees and mountains

8 You may make this before painting.

space	frame	canvas
dissatisfied	sculptor	landscape
beautiful	exhibition	sketch
prodigy	dishonest	

B Circle the correct words and complete the sentences with the words in the box.

pastels	surrounded	street painter
perspective	talented	three-dimensional

Will / Shall (1) I tell you about my day yesterday? I met **a / the** (2) ____________ (3)! He was drawing a sketch of **the / a** (4) canyon on the sidewalk. It looked ____________ (5), and he was so much fun to watch! He didn't have **everything / anything** (6) to drink, so I said, "**Shall I / I'll** (7) get you a soda." I ran to the supermarket on the corner. When I came back, he was ____________ (8) by people! **Anyone / Everyone** (9) was taking his picture. He painted in pretty ____________ (10), and he added shading and ____________ (11) to the painting. When he finished, I stepped onto **the / a** (12) painting! He was really ____________ (13)!

C Complete the sentences with the word pairs in the box.

shading–contrast	complex–speechless	ignored–sketch	shapes–string

1 Sumin cut out interesting ____________. She attached them with ____________.

2 Karl took a pencil. He added ____________ and ____________ to the sketch.

3 Paula ____________ the mistakes she made. She gave the ____________ to Sam.

4 Ben finished his ____________ painting. He gave it to Tara, who was ____________!

D Join the sentences from C to make one sentence.

1 Sumin cut out interesting shapes and attached them with string.

2 ____________

3 ____________

4 ____________

BIG QUESTION 5

What is a city?

Think and write.

What do you know?

____

____

____

____

____

____

____

____

____

What do you want to know?

____

____

____

____

____

____

____

____

____

UNIT 9 Get Ready

Words

A Read and number.

1 batik
2 rickshaw
3 exotic fruits
4 architecture
5 souvenirs
6 street vendor
7 antiques
8 shrimp
9 tuna
10 port
11 canal

☐ 

☐ 

☐ 

☐ 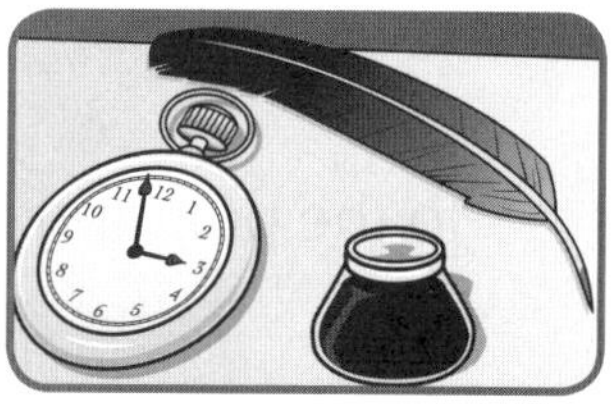

☐ 

☐ 

☐ 

☐ 

☐ 

☐ 

☐ 

B Two of the words are correct. Cross out the wrong word.

1 This can move around.

a rickshaw b ~~architecture~~ c street vendor

2 This lives under water.

a antiques b tuna c shrimp

3 This holds water for transportation.

a port b canal c street vendor

4 This is often colorful.

a canal b batik c exotic fruit

5 People sometimes buy and collect these.

a souvenirs b shrimp c antiques

6 Someone designed or created this.

a exotic fruits b architecture c batik

C Complete the sentences with the words in the box.

souvenirs	shrimp	rickshaw	architecture	exotic fruits	canals

I had a wonderful time in Bangkok, Thailand, today. First, a friendly man gave me a ride in his ________ (1). He was strong and pulled me easily. I then took a boat ride on the Chao Phraya River and on some small ________ (2). After a quick lunch, I went shopping and bought some Thai ________ (3). Then, I took a bus tour to see some interesting Bangkok ________ (4), such as the Elephant Building and the Robot Building. Tonight, I had a delicious dinner of ________ (5) curry and rice, and then some ________ (6) for dessert.

Read

A Read the article. What are some things that make Lisbon an interesting city?

____

____

B Read again. As you read, try to paraphrase sentences that contain main ideas or important facts.

Lisbon, a European Port City

Lisbon, the capital city of Portugal, is one of the oldest cities in the world. It is older than Rome, Paris, or London. At one time, Romans and Arabs ruled there. Today, Lisbon has one of the largest **ports** in Europe. It has a population of three million people.

Visiting Lisbon

Lisbon is an exciting and historic city. It has mild winters and very warm summers. The city is on seven hills, and it has charming streets with white limestone buildings. If you like famous **architecture**, visit the St. George Castle. You can also visit the Vasco da Gama Bridge. It is the longest bridge in Europe.

Getting Around

There are buses, trains, taxis, and trams throughout the city. If the weather is good, a bicycle is more enjoyable. Take a bike ride along the Tagus River on the Poetry Bike Lane. It goes from Baixa to Belem. Belem is famous for the beautiful Belem Tower and the Jerónimos Monastery. Belem also has an **antique** market twice a month.

Think Paraphrase one of the sentences in the paragraphs above.

Sightseeing, Shopping, and Eating

Rossio is the main square in Lisbon. It is an interesting place to visit. For great shopping, check out Baixa and the Chiado. In addition, **street vendors** sell **souvenirs** and other items. If you are hungry, restaurants serve delicious seafood such as cod, **shrimp**, and **tuna**. In fact, people in Lisbon eat more fish than anyone else in Europe.

Think Paraphrase the paragraph above.

No one could ever be bored in Lisbon. Whatever you like, there is something interesting for you to enjoy there.

Student Book page 89

Comprehension

A **If you could go to Lisbon for a weekend, what would you do? Write two things you would do and your reasons.**

____

____

B **Write a paraphrased sentence for each set of two sentences below.**

1 There are buses, trains, taxis, and trams throughout the city. If the weather is good, a bicycle is more enjoyable.

You can travel around Lisbon by bus, train, taxi, tram, or even bicycle.

2 If you like famous architecture, visit the St. George Castle. You can also visit the Vasco da Gama Bridge.

____

3 Take a bike ride along the Tagus River on the Poetry Bike Lane. It goes from Baixa to Belem.

____

C **Write three things that make Lisbon special.**

1 ______________________________

2 ______________________________

3 ______________________________

D **Words in Context** **Read and write.**

countless	congested	haggle	banned

1 A bicycle is a good way to travel when traffic in a city is ____________ .

2 In some antique markets, you can ____________ over the selling price.

3 Throughout Lisbon, cheap and tasty restaurants are ____________ .

4 Some old cars that pollute a lot are ____________ from the city center.

Student Book page 92

Grammar in Use

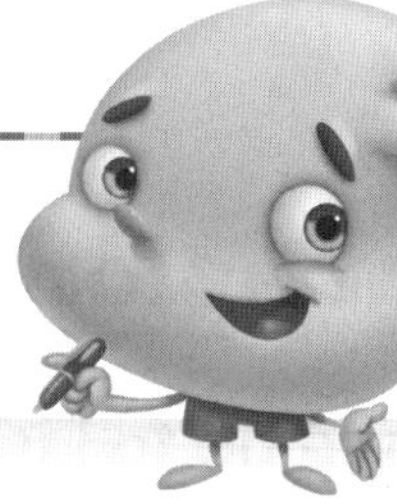

A Study the grammar.

Learn Negative Indefinite Pronouns

Negative Indefinite Pronoun	Meaning	Example
nothing	no single thing, not anything	There was **nothing** in the central market that I wanted to buy.
no one	no person	**No one** could ever be bored in Lisbon.
nobody		There was **nobody** at the city information desk.

Do not use another negative in a sentence with *nothing*, *no one*, or *nobody*.
He ~~didn't buy~~ **nothing** the entire day. (X)
He **bought** **nothing** the entire day. (O)

B Read and write.

1 Nobody drove a car after the snowstorm.

2 There is ______________ else at the restaurant.

3 There is ______________ in my pockets.

C Complete the sentences with *nothing* or *no one* / *nobody*.

1 There was ______________ that looked fresh at the fruit stand.

2 ______________ was waiting at the bus stop when I arrived.

3 ______________ in my father's company drives to work. They all take the train.

4 There was ______________ to do outside on a rainy day, so we went to the library.

Student Book page 93

D Circle the correct pronoun.

Yesterday, my mom and I went shopping in the city. There is **nothing** / **anything** (1) better than shopping in a big department store! First, I asked all of my friends to go with me, but **anyone** / **no one** (2) was able to go. Mom looked through all the stores, but she didn't buy **nothing** / **anything** (3) for herself. However, she bought **nothing** / **something** (4) for me. It was a new jacket! **Nobody** / **Anybody** (5) knows about it, so I'll surprise my friends and wear it tomorrow.

E Correct the sentences using negative indefinite pronouns.

1 There isn't nothing interesting to see at the cinema.

There is nothing interesting to see at the cinema.

2 There wasn't nobody in the restaurant after 1:00 p.m.

3 I haven't got nothing to do, so let's go to the science museum.

4 No one didn't find the keys that I lost at the department store.

F Rewrite each sentence with a negative indefinite pronoun.

1 I didn't buy anything at the antique market this morning.

I bought nothing at the antique market this morning.

2 There isn't anybody riding a bicycle along the river today.

3 My little brother doesn't eat anything that has shrimp in it.

Communicate

Word Study

commerce   corner   cinema   cement   castle   ceiling

A Read. Circle the bolded words that begin with a *soft c*. Underline the bolded words that begin with a *hard c*. Then match.

1 Many **cinemas** play more than one movie at a time, so people can choose what they want to see.

2 **Cement** is a necessary part of a city since people use it to make roads, sidewalks, and buildings.

3 Many old cities in Europe have **castles** that people built centuries ago.

4 When people go shopping in a large city, they are helping **commerce** grow there.

5 Carlos waited for the bus on a street **corner**.

6 Water is dripping from the **ceiling**.

a 

b 

c 

d 

e 

f 

B Complete the sentences. Use the words in the box.

Cities are always busy. Of course, cities have a lot of ______________ (1), with people buying and selling everywhere. You can also see trucks carrying ______________ (2) and other supplies for new buildings and roads. In my city, they just finished building a new ______________ (3) on the ______________ (4) of Main Street and 2nd Avenue. They built it to look like a ______________ (5) from the Middle Ages. The ______________ (6) in the lobby is filled with bright lights that look like stars.

Writing Study

A **Read the sentences. Capitalize the names of the bodies of water. Then rewrite the sentences.**

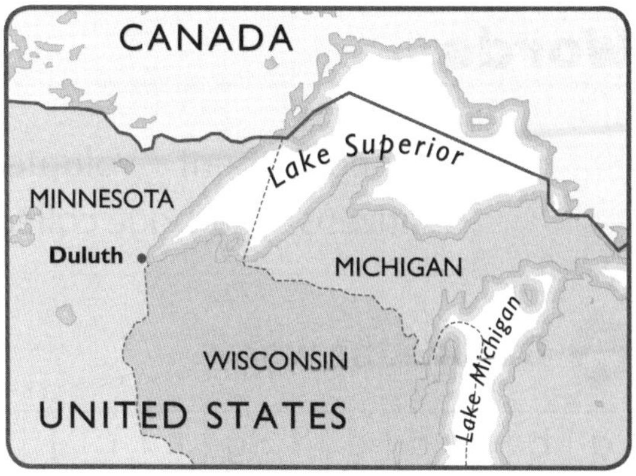

1 Lake superior is the most western of the great lakes, reaching the city of Duluth.

Lake Superior is the most western of the Great Lakes, reaching the city of Duluth.

2 The arctic ocean is the smallest of the world's five oceans.

3 The island of Dominica in the caribbean sea has a lake called boiling lake.

4 The congo river flows past the city of Kinshasa as it heads to the atlantic ocean.

5 The panama canal reaches the pacific ocean at Panama City.

B **Write a paragraph about a city near water that you would like to visit. Write at least one sentence with a negative indefinite pronoun. Be sure to capitalize the names of bodies of water.**

I would like to visit the city of Manaus in the Amazon rainforest of Brazil. You can find this city where the **Negro River** and **Solimoes River** come together. Manaus has a famous opera house called the Teatro Amazonas. **Nobody** in my class likes opera, but I do!

UNIT 10 Get Ready

Words

equipment volunteers playground news conference city hall
citizens garbage collectors mayor president city council assistant

A Decode the words.

a	b	c	d	e	f	g	h	i	j	k	l	m	n	o	p	q	r	s	t	u	v	w	x	y	z
1	2	3	4	5	6	7	8	9	10	11	12	13	14	15	16	17	18	19	20	21	22	23	24	25	26

1 ___ ___ ___ ___ ___ ___ ___
7 1 18 2 1 7 5
___ ___ ___ ___ ___ ___ ___ ___ ___ ___
3 15 12 12 5 3 20 15 18 19

2 ___ ___ ___ ___ ___
13 1 25 15 18

3 ___ ___ ___ ___ ___ ___ ___ ___ ___
5 17 21 9 16 13 5 14 20

4 ___ ___ ___ ___ ___ ___ ___ ___ ___
1 19 19 9 19 20 1 14 20

5 ___ ___ ___ ___ ___ ___ ___ ___
3 9 20 9 26 5 14 19

6 ___ ___ ___ ___
3 9 20 25
___ ___ ___ ___ ___ ___ ___
3 15 21 14 3 9 12

7 ___ ___ ___ ___ ___ ___ ___ ___
3 9 20 25 8 1 12 12

8 ___ ___ ___ ___ ___ ___ ___ ___ ___ ___
16 12 1 25 7 18 15 21 14 4

9 ___ ___ ___ ___ ___ ___ ___ ___ ___
16 18 5 19 9 4 5 14 20

10 ___ ___ ___ ___ ___ ___ ___ ___ ___ ___
22 15 12 21 14 20 5 5 18 19

11 ___ ___ ___ ___ ___ ___ ___ ___ ___ ___ ___ ___ ___ ___
14 5 23 19 3 15 14 6 5 18 5 14 3 5

B Look and write.

1

____

2

____

3

____

4
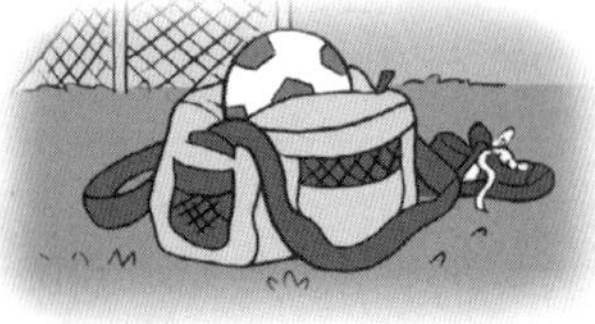
____

5

____

6

____

equipment volunteers playground news conference city hall citizens garbage collectors mayor president ~~city council~~ assistant

C Fill in the chart with the words in the box.

People	Places	Things
city council		

D Complete the sentences with the words in the box.

1 The ______________ of our city held a ______________ yesterday. There were many people there from the city newspapers and television stations.

2 Patricia's father is the ______________ of a company. He is very busy, so he has an ______________ to help him with all of his meetings and paperwork.

3 José is one of many ______________ of his city. He works hard all week, but he is also happy to be one of the ______________ at the city's youth center.

4 Our ______________ is a beautiful building made of granite. The ______________ meets with the mayor there once a week.

5 The vast ______________ in our city park is very safe for children, and the ______________ in it is new. The park is also very clean, since ______________ come by every afternoon to pick up the trash.

Read

A **Read. How does a parade show us what a city is like?**

B **Read again. As you read, ask yourself about the main character and minor characters in the story. Try to understand what they're like.**

Mayor for Another Day!

Marcy was reading a book at home when her mother rushed in. "The mayor phoned!" she said. "He wants to see you!"

Marcy biked to the **city hall**. Mayor Wilson and the **city council** looked worried. "People are staying at home with their computers," said the mayor. "They don't go out into the city."

"They aren't going to the zoo or to art galleries," said Miss Martinez, the head of the council. "They aren't going to concerts or sports games or restaurants."

"It's an emergency!" cried Mayor Wilson. "I'm missing my tuba lesson to be here."

Marcy snapped her fingers. "You gave me an idea, Mr. Mayor." She quickly explained her plan.

Think
Who is the main character? What is she like?

The next Saturday morning, Marcy waited nervously outside with her mother. Soon they heard music! Two girls appeared holding a banner. It said "Glenview City Appreciation Day!" After them came a colorful parade. The city band marched and played with Mayor Wilson and his tuba. Cages filled with zoo animals rolled by. Company **presidents**, **garbage collectors**, dancers, artists, and athletes marched proudly, while chefs from the restaurants handed out food. Crowds of excited people came out of their homes to watch.

"We live in a great city, don't we?" Marcy's mother asked.

Marcy nodded happily. Her plan was working!

By the next week, the zoo, the **playgrounds**, the sports stadium, the concert halls, the art galleries, and the restaurants were full of Glenview **citizens**.

Mayor Wilson called Marcy. "You're a hero!" he exclaimed.

"It was my pleasure," Marcy said.

Think
Who are the minor characters? What are they like?

Student Book page 97

Comprehension

A Write two things you liked about "Mayor for Another Day!"

____

____

B Complete the chart with the words in the box. Then write whether the sentence describes a *strength* or a *weakness*.

~~Marcy~~	Mayor Wilson	artists	chefs	citizens

	Character	Strength / Weakness
1 She has many creative ideas.	Marcy	strength
2 They didn't want to go out and do things.		
3 They are proud to show their art at galleries.		
4 They do their best to cook delicious food.		
5 He is not afraid to ask for help.		

C Answer the questions.

1 What can happen when people spend all their time on computers?

____

2 What can happen to zoos, art galleries, and restaurants when nobody goes there?

____

3 What did the city parade remind people about?

____

D **Words in Context** Read and write.

members	contest	speech	ribbon

1 After the parade, Mayor Wilson gave a ______________ in front of city hall.

2 Glenview won a national ______________ this year for the most interesting city.

3 The Glenview city council has seven ______________, including Miss Martinez.

4 After his speech, Mayor Wilson gave Marcy a ______________ for helping the city.

Student Book page 100

Grammar in Use

A Study the grammar.

Learn **Tag Questions**

We	**live** / **don't live**	in a great city,	**don't** / **do**	we?	
The garbage collectors	**didn't have** / **had**	a holiday last week,	**did** / **didn't**	they?	
You	**will go** / **won't go**	to the town meeting tonight,	**won't** / **will**	you?	
Mayor Wilson	**can** / **can't**	play the tuba,	**can't** / **can**	he?	

B Underline the subject in the statement. Then circle its pronoun in the tag.

1 A city usually has lots of hotels for visitors, doesn't (it?)

2 Sushi restaurants are popular in Tokyo, aren't they?

3 The mayor will be in the parade tomorrow, won't she?

4 The soccer team didn't win the game last night, did it?

5 Thomas can visit the art museum this afternoon, can't he?

6 The garbage collectors don't work tomorrow, do they?

C Circle the correct tag question.

1 A city needs playgrounds for children, **doesn't it** / **don't they**?

2 The city council didn't meet last night, **didn't it** / **did it**?

3 The artists will have an exhibition next week, **won't it** / **won't they**?

4 Charlie doesn't play in the city orchestra, **does he** / **do they**?

5 The koala at the city zoo is a quiet animal, **was it** / **isn't it**?

6 The chefs at this restaurant can cook well, **can't they** / **can he**?

Student Book page 101

D Rewrite the sentence with the correct tag question.

1 You enjoy looking at interesting architecture, do you?

You enjoy looking at interesting architecture, don't you?

2 Sandra didn't take a boat ride on the canal, does she?

____

3 The mayor will have a news conference tomorrow, won't it?

____

4 Volunteers can paint the equipment, can't it?

____

E Complete each sentence with the correct tag question.

1 Seoul is a very interesting place to live, ______________________________?

2 The playground doesn't have new equipment, ______________________________?

3 The city council members will decide soon, ______________________________?

4 The city band didn't play that song before, ______________________________?

F Read. Then write a sentence with a tag question.

1 You think Istanbul is the largest city in Europe, but you're not sure.

Istanbul is the largest city in Europe, isn't it?

2 You think the city council wants to build a new playground, but you're not sure.

____

____

3 You think the Chicago City Hall burned down in 1871, but you're not sure.

____

4 You think your city's baseball team will win the game, but you're not sure.

____

Communicate

Word Study

take down	take in	take after	take over	take up	take apart

A **Complete the sentences with the phrasal verbs in the box. Use the correct tense. Then number.**

1 The bus mechanic ____________ the engine and put it back together again.

2 After the circus left, the workers ____________ the posters around the city.

3 Nora is a ballet dancer, but she wants to ____________ jazz dancing, too.

4 It was hard for Vicente to ____________ all the sights and sounds of the city.

5 The mayor's assistant ____________ in the office when the mayor is out.

6 Karim ____________ his father. They both enjoy watching soccer.

☐ 

☐ 

☐ 

☐ 

☐ 

☐ 

B **Complete the sentences with the phrasal verbs in the box. Use the correct tense.**

My older sister will move to Sao Paulo tomorrow to study at a university. She was very busy today. First, she ____________ (1) all of the posters in her bedroom. Then she ____________ (2) her bicycle because it won't fit in the car. She's very excited to go. She ____________ (3) our mother, who also loves new adventures. My sister plans to ____________ (4) many new hobbies and sports at school. What about me? Well, I'll ____________ (5) as the oldest child in the house now. It's a lot to ____________ (6), but I'm excited to help my parents more. I'm also looking forward to having my own bedroom while my sister is gone!

Student Book page 103

Writing Study

A **Complete each sentence with *and*, *but*, or *or*.**

1 I could live in a large town __________ in a city, but not in the countryside.

2 A city can be an expensive place to live, __________ there are good jobs there.

3 Jenna cleaned her apartment __________ went shopping in the city on the same day.

4 You can go to the concert on Friday, __________ you can't go on Saturday.

5 They will either eat at the Russian restaurant __________ at the Chinese restaurant.

6 Company presidents __________ garbage collectors both have important jobs.

7 The city had money to build a new zoo __________ a new concert hall, but not both.

8 Every person who lives in a city is a citizen, __________ not everyone is a volunteer.

B **Write a paragraph about what you enjoy in a city. Write at least one sentence with a tag question. Be sure to use sentences with the coordinating conjunctions *and*, *but*, or *or*.**

International restaurants are great places to eat, aren't they? Cities have more international restaurants than towns do. In my city, you can eat food from Europe, the Middle East, Africa, Asia, **or** South America. I usually have a main dish **and** dessert, **but** I always try to eat healthy food.

Writing

A Read this persuasive essay about the writer's city. Label the parts of the report.

Sydney, Australia

Did you know that Sydney, Australia, is called one of the world's most beautiful cities? There are three reasons why you should live here.

Some people may think that Australian cities aren't cosmopolitan. However, Sydney is one of the most cosmopolitan cities in the world. Thirty percent of the citizens of Sydney were born in another country.

Do you think that city architecture is all the same? Then come to Sydney! We have some of the most interesting architecture in the world. Sydney is famous for the Sydney Opera House as well as the Sydney Harbour Bridge.

You may think that cities are separate from nature. However, this is not true in Sydney. You can see whales near our coasts and beautiful birds in our trees. You can even see kangaroos in our Royal National Park.

Come to Sydney for its cosmopolitan life, its architecture, and its nature. You will soon understand why it is my favorite city in the world.

B Plan your persuasive essay about your city or town. Write three reasons why someone should live there. Then write three reasons why someone may choose not to live there.

My City or Town	
Why Someone Should Live There	**Why Someone May Choose Not to Live There**

C Now go to your notebook to write your own persuasive essay about why people should live in your city or town. Then read and revise it.

My writing checklist:

- ☐ In my introduction paragraph, I included my reason for writing.
- ☐ In the body, I explained how the reader may disagree with me. Then I gave reasons why he or she should agree with me.
- ☐ In my conclusion paragraph, I summarized my main ideas.

Student Book page 104

What did you learn?

BIG QUESTION 5

What is a city?

Review

A Circle True (T) or False (F).

1 A rickshaw stays in one place. T F

2 Garbage collectors help keep a city clean. T F

3 Canals have water in them. T F

4 You can see a live play at a cinema. T F

5 A city council can make decisions about a city. T F

6 Street vendors can sell food. T F

B Complete the sentences with the word pairs in the box.

volunteers–take down
president–news conference took over–congested
shrimp–tuna mayor–members

1 It takes a lot of ____________ to equal the weight of one ____________ .

2 James ____________ the job of reducing the city's ____________ traffic.

3 The ____________ helped to ____________ the decorations after the parade.

4 The ____________ thanked the ____________ of his city council.

5 The ____________ held a ____________ to introduce her company's products.

C Rewrite each sentence. Capitalize the names of bodies of water and add a tag question.

1 The mississippi river flows into the gulf of mexico. **The Mississippi River flows into the Gulf of Mexico, doesn't it?**

2 Lake baikal is the oldest and deepest freshwater lake. ______________________________

3 The nile river flows north into the mediterranean sea. ______________________________

4 Peru and Bolivia share lake titicaca's resources. ______________________________

D Circle the correct words in each sentence.

1 The city council had **nothing** / **nobody** to decide, **and** / **but** they met at city hall anyway.

2 The market had many antiques **or** / **and** souvenirs, but I saw **nobody** / **nothing** that I wanted.

3 **No one** / **Nothing** in my class won a ribbon at the speech contest, **and** / **but** we had fun anyway.

4 The city banned all cars **or** / **and** trucks in the tourist area, so **nobody** / **nothing** can drive there.

E Complete the sentences with the words in the box. You won't use some words.

or	they	nothing	nobody	and	won't	it	will

1 There was ______________ at the port at 8:00 p.m. Not one person was there.

2 Commerce is very important for the health of a city, isn't ______________ ?

3 We have two choices. We can go to the zoo, ______________ we can go to the art museum.

4 It will take a few hours to take apart the equipment, ______________ it?

5 The mayor's assistant can do anything. There's ______________ she can't do.

BIG QUESTION 6

How do our bodies work?

Think and write.

What do you know?

What do you want to know?

Student Book pages 106–108

Words

A Unscramble and write the words. Then solve the secret message.

commoncold	microscope	paralyze	bacteria	
influenza	cells	infect	disease	virus

Scrambled word	Boxes	Numbered letters
citefn	6 boxes	2nd box: 9; 6th box: 2
smrecpoioc	10 boxes	6th box: 1
teabiacr	8 boxes	2nd box: 10; 4th box: 6
llces	5 boxes	2nd box: 13
monmoc lodc	6 boxes + 4 boxes	6th box: 11; 8th box: 8; 10th box: 12
zylreapa	8 boxes	4th box: 14; 6th box: 4
sesidea	7 boxes	3rd box: 5
sivru	5 boxes	3rd box: 7
lunneizaf	9 boxes	4th box: 15; 9th box: 3

Secret Message

_ _ _ _
1 2 3 4

_ _ _ _ _ g
5 6 7 8 9

_ _ _
10 11 12

h _ _ _ _ h _ !
13 14 15 2 4

B Circle the correct answers.

1 The scientist could easily see the bacteria through the **microscope** / **cell**.

2 People often get **immune** / **influenza** in the winter.

3 It's possible for a person with influenza to **paralyze** / **infect** others.

4 People often catch the **common cold** / **mucus** many times in their lives.

5 New medicines can help people fight **diseases** / **cells**.

6 Some **viruses** / **bacteria** are necessary for life on Earth.

C Complete the sentences with the words in the box.

microscope	infect	influenza	immune	virus

A few weeks ago, I had ______(1)______. I had a high fever and my body hurt, so my mom took me to the doctor. He said that a(n) ______(2)______ caused me to get sick. He told me I had to stay home for five days. I didn't want to ______(3)______ anyone else. My sister never gets sick, so perhaps she is ______(4)______ to this type of virus. Later, I did some research about influenza. I saw a picture on the Internet of an influenza virus. A scientist used a powerful ______(5)______ to get the picture. It looked dangerous!

D Circle True (T) or False (F).

1 A person can't walk if an accident paralyzes his or her legs. T F

2 Too much mucus can make breathing through your nose difficult. T F

3 Plants don't have cells. T F

4 Bacteria are always good for us. T F

5 People with a common cold sometimes sneeze. T F

6 Disease can make humans, animals, and plants sick. T F

A Read the diary. What is the virus trying to do?

B Read the diary again. As you read, think about the main ideas and the theme of the story.

Diary of a Virus

Monday, January 21

As a **virus** for the **common cold**, life can be difficult. For example, I tried to **infect** a boy in elementary school throughout the day. His name is Sam. I waited on his desktop, and when he touched the desk I jumped on his finger. Unfortunately, Sam didn't touch his eyes, mouth, or nose. Then, right after class, he washed his hands. Now I'm full of soap and sitting in a sink!

Think
What is the main idea of the reading so far?

Tuesday, January 22

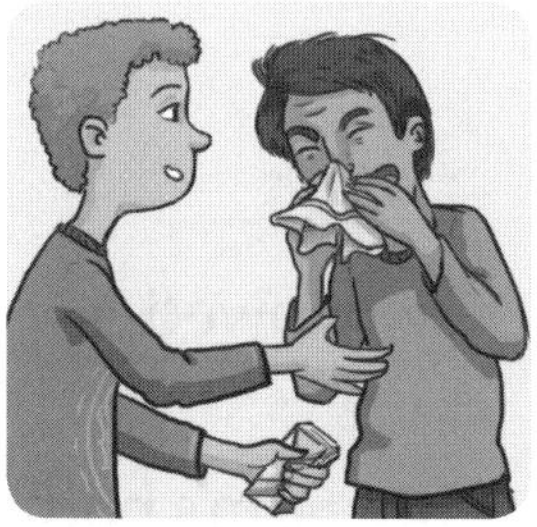

This morning I jumped into the nose of Sam's best friend, Bill. Unfortunately, the **mucus** in his nose caught me. I thought it was over for me, when suddenly Bill sneezed while he was talking to Sam. I knew that would send me right into Sam's face! However, Sam quickly gave Bill a tissue, and Bill sneezed into that instead! Infecting people is harder than I imagined.

Wednesday, January 23

I'm feeling very unhappy today. Some scientists caught my friend Harry and put him under a **microscope**. Harry is an **influenza** virus, and he's a dangerous little guy. Anyway, Sam ate all his vegetables today, he's exercising, and he's getting eight hours of sleep every night. His body is too strong for me!

Thursday, January 24

I tried to infect Sam again today, but he washed his hands five times and never touched his face! He also gave tissues to every student in his class who was sneezing. It's impossible to give him a cold! I give up. I'm moving to another school.

Think
What is another main idea in the reading?

Understand

Comprehension

A **Did you find "Diary of a Virus" funny or interesting? Why or why not? Write your ideas and your reasons.**

____

____

B **Circle the best choice for the story's main idea and theme.**

1 Main idea:

a Wash your hands with soap every day to kill viruses.

b There are many ways to stop a virus from infecting you.

c Give tissues to everyone who is sneezing when they have a cold.

2 Theme:

a Viruses feel happy, sad, and angry, just as people do.

b Be a good friend when other people around you are sick.

c It is important to protect your own body against viruses.

C **Answer the questions.**

1 What should you do after touching things in school?

____

2 Why are tissues important when you sneeze?

____

3 What can healthy food, exercise, and enough sleep do for your body?

____

D **Words in Context** **Read and write.**

suit	scrape	fluids	swallowed

1 Mucus and tears are both ______________ that Sam's body makes.

2 If Bill ______________ the virus, he might catch a cold.

3 Fortunately, Sam didn't have a ______________ on his hands for the virus to get in.

4 Your skin can act like a ______________ of armor to protect you from viruses.

Grammar in Use

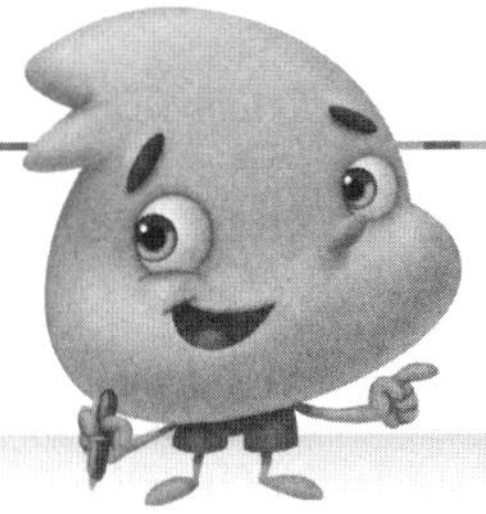

A Study the grammar.

Learn **Order of Adjectives**

opinion ➜	size ➜	age ➜	shape ➜	color ➜	kind
interesting	*little*	*young*	*round*	*blue*	*metal*

Harry is an influenza virus, and he's a **dangerous little** guy.
(opinion) (size)

Can you see the **tiny**, **round**, **green** virus in the microscope?
(size) (shape) (color)

This **square**, **white**, **metal** box contains an important medicine to fight bacteria.
(shape) (color) (kind)

B **Read. Then name the adjectives.**

1 Jeremy swallowed the (a) awful-tasting, (b) pink, (c) liquid medicine.

a opinion b color c kind

2 The nurse cleaned the (a) painful, (b) little, (c) red scrape on Ann's hand.

a ______ b ______ c ______

3 This (a) powerful, (b) new, (c) influezna-fighting medicine paralyzes the virus.

a ______ b ______ c ______

4 That (a) old, (b) gray, (c) metal microscope belonged to my grandfather.

a ______ b ______ c ______

C **Complete the sentences with the adjectives in the box.**

green	tiny	cotton	young

1 I wore a blue ______ T-shirt when I went to the clinic.

2 This round, ______ cold virus looks very interesting under the microscope.

3 The kind, ______ doctor checked the little girl for influenza.

4 Scientists discovered some interesting, ______, new bacteria today.

D Rewrite each sentence with the underlined adjectives in the correct order.

1 The medicine attacked the blue, dangerous, new virus.

2 This tiny, green, rectangular plant cell has very thick walls.

3 The young, tall, curious student made an important discovery.

4 Liz sprayed the cup-shaped, yellow, beautiful flowers to protect them from animals.

E Unscramble the sentences. Then number.

1 good-tasting / gave / Ben / medicine / red / Dr. Garcia / some

2 viruses / can / electron / powerful / see / microscope / This

3 cotton / This / stop / can / mask / viruses / simple

☐ 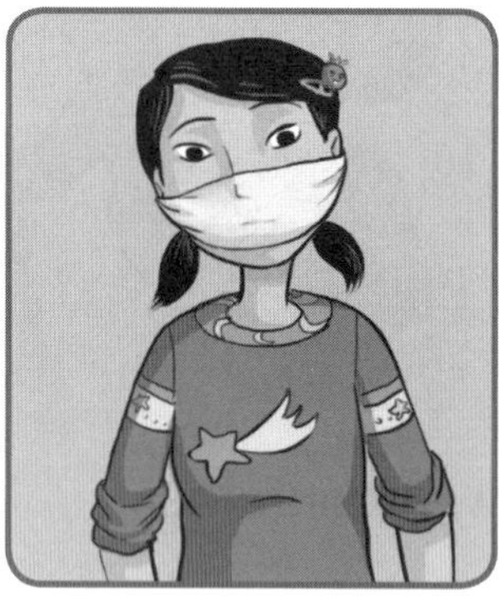

☐ 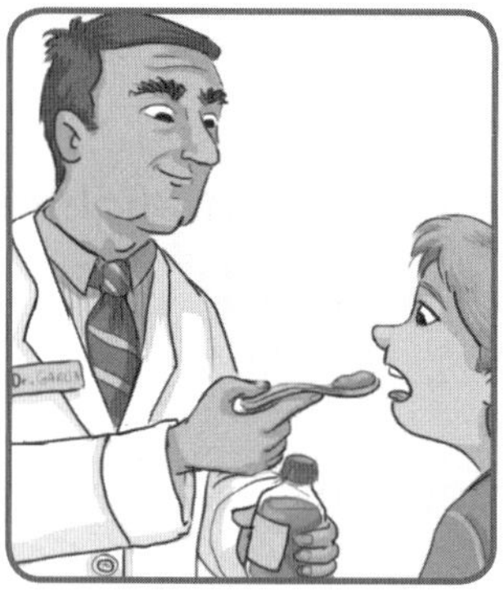

☐ 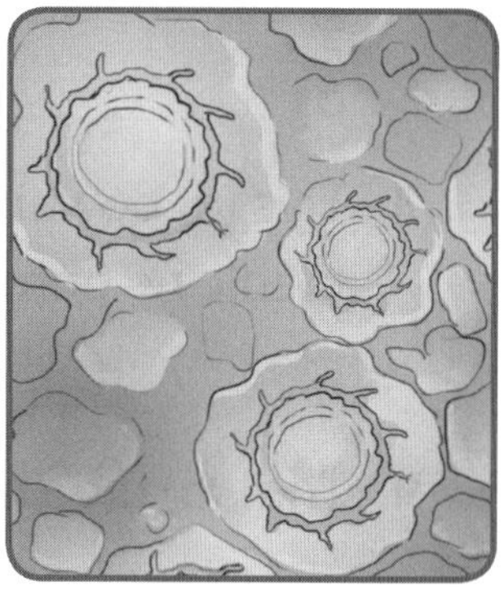

F Write sentences. Use two or three adjectives.

1 Describe something that you own.

I own a sporty, new, red bicycle.

2 Describe something in nature that you saw today.

3 Describe something that you are wearing now.

Word Study

shrink live inhale dead expand exhale

A **Look and write.**

1 

____

2 

____

3 

____

4 

____

5 

____

6 

____

B **Complete the sentences with the words in the box. Use the correct tense of the verbs.**

1 They ______________ the nurse's office at our school. It now has four beds instead of two. Unfortunately, they had to ______________ the size of the cafeteria to do this.

2 The top layer of your skin is made of ______________ cells. Since they aren't living, they stop viruses from getting into your body. However, when you have a cut, some of your ______________ cells are open to the air, and viruses can get in.

3 When you sneeze, you first ______________ air into your body quickly. Then, even more quickly, you ______________ it out of your body!

Student Book page 115

Writing Study

A **Read. Then write a negative command and a positive command.**

1 Your friend is going to sneeze into the air. What should you say?

Don't sneeze into the air. Sneeze into a tissue.

2 Your friend isn't feeling well in the classroom but doesn't want to go to the nurse's office. What should you say?

3 Your friend has dirty hands and is holding a sandwich. What should you say?

4 Your friend goes to bed every night at 11:30 p.m. What should you say?

5 Your friend plays computer games and never exercises. What should you say?

B **Read. Then write a paragraph about good health habits. Write at least one sentence with two or three adjectives. Be sure to write commands that explain what to do or what not to do.**

How can you stay healthy during the cold and flu season? **Eat** a diet with lots of vegetables. **Eat leafy, green** vegetables such as spinach and kale. **Don't forget** to eat **delicious, colorful** vegetables such as carrots and peppers, too. **Wash** your vegetables before you eat them.

Words

lungs	blood	system	carbon dioxide	arteries	
capillaries	pulse	heart	veins	diaphragm	trachea

A Look and write.

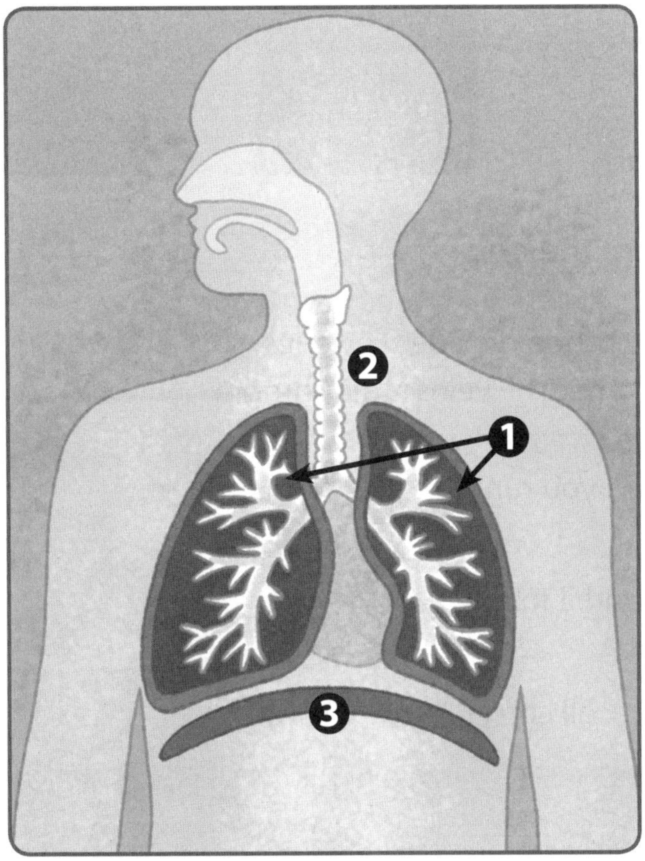

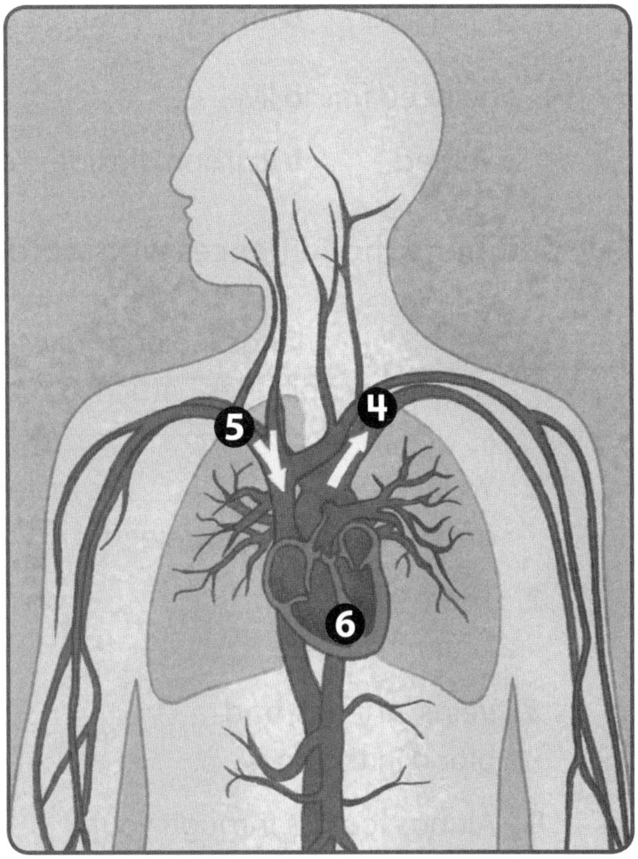

1 ______________________

2 ______________________

3 ______________________

4 ______________________

5 ______________________

6 ______________________

B Complete the sentences with the words in the box.

1 Each of the illustrations above shows a ______________ in the body.

2 It is quite easy to feel your ______________ in your wrists and in your neck.

3 Plants need ______________, and humans need oxygen.

4 Red ______________ flows through every part of the body.

5 ______________ are smaller than arteries and veins.

Student Book page 116

C Two of the three words are correct. Cross out the wrong word.

1 You only have one of these in your body.

a heart **b** lung **c** diaphragm

2 Outside air goes into this part of your body.

a lung **b** trachea **c** capillaries

3 This carries blood in your body.

a trachea **b** artery **c** vein

4 You need this to live.

a blood **b** carbon dioxide **c** heart

D Complete the sentences with words from the box.

lungs	blood	system	carbon dioxide	arteries	
capillaries	trachea	pulse	heart	veins	diaphragm

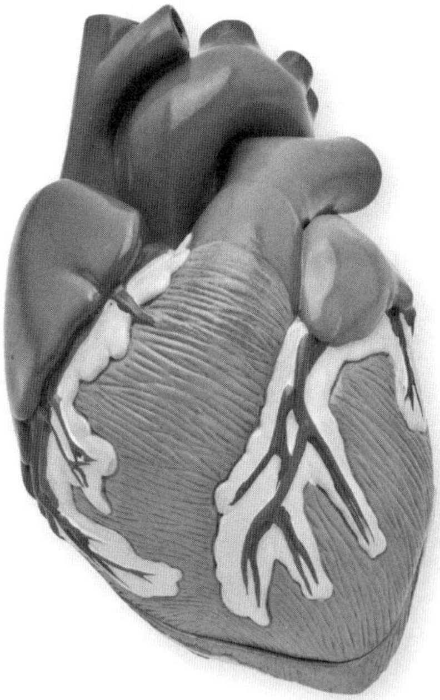

1 Your ________________ is faster when you run and slower when you sleep.

2 There is ________________ on my hand. I think I cut my finger.

3 Veins, arteries, and ________________ all carry blood in the body.

4 Air has to pass through your ________________ before it enters your lungs.

5 The ________________ is in the chest, a little to the left of the center.

6 Humans breathe out ________________, which plants need to live.

7 All the ________________ in the body carry blood back to the heart.

8 You have two ________________, one on each side of your chest.

9 It would be difficult to breathe in and out without the ________________.

10 Our lungs, trachea, and diaphragm work together as a ________________.

11 The ________________ carry blood to every part of the body.

Read

A **Read the article. How is exercise good for your body?**

____

____

B **Read the article again. As you read, remember to look for clue words that help you understand the sequence of the actions in the reading.**

What Happens When You Exercise?

People used to think that exercise was just for athletes. We now know that exercise is important for everyone. When you exercise, your muscles get stronger. You also become more flexible, and you feel better. However, what happens inside your body when you exercise?

Imagine that you decide to jog around the park for thirty minutes. When you begin to run, your muscles start working hard. As a result, they need more oxygen. Then, two things happen.

> **Think**
> What is the sequence of actions up to now?

First, your breathing increases. This sends more oxygen through your trachea and into your **lungs**. During this time, your **diaphragm** is working harder to let your lungs expand and shrink faster. Next, your **heart** beats faster. It sends more oxygen-rich blood through your **arteries** to your muscles. Your muscles then use the oxygen. In fact, your muscles use most of the oxygen that your body brings in when you exercise. Of course, after your body uses oxygen, it produces **carbon dioxide**. This travels back through your **veins** and out of your lungs into the air.

> **Think**
> What is the sequence of actions in this paragraph?

While this is happening, your skin produces a clear fluid called *sweat*. It keeps your body from becoming too hot. Your body also keeps you cool by sending blood to your skin. This gives your skin a healthy glow.

After you stop running, your muscles need much less oxygen. Your breathing and heart rate return to normal, and your body now feels great! Exercising is a good way to keep your body strong and fit.

Understand

Comprehension

A **What did you learn about your body and exercise? Write two things you learned.**

____

____

B **Number the actions.**

Step One	**Step Two**
____ Your muscles need more oxygen. ____ Your muscles start working hard. __1__ You begin to run.	____ Your lungs expand and shrink faster. __4__ The diaphragm works harder. ____ More oxygen enters your lungs.
Step Three	**Step Four**
__7__ Your heart beats faster. ____ Your muscles use this oxygen. ____ Oxygen-rich blood goes to your muscles.	____ Your breathing and heart rate return to normal. __10__ You stop running. ____ Your muscles need less oxygen.

C **Answer the questions.**

1 What does your body produce after it uses oxygen?

____

2 Why is sweat important?

____

3 After you stop exercising, what happens to your heart?

____

D **Words in Context** Read and write.

major pumps tubes squeezes

1 The heart ______________ blood throughout the entire body.

2 The diaphragm ______________ the lungs so that a person can exhale.

3 The heart and lungs are two ______________ parts of the body.

4 Arteries and veins are ______________ that carry blood.

Grammar in Use

A Study the grammar.

Learn *Used To*

Repeated Action in the Past	Single Action in the Past
He **used to exercise** all the time.	He **exercised** last week.
The children **used to run** a mile every day for exercise.	The children **ran** a mile yesterday.
People **used to think** that exercise was just for athletes.	Fifty years ago, people **thought** that exercise was just for athletes.

B **Match the two parts of each sentence. Underline *used to* in each sentence. Circle the verb after *used to*.**

1 I used to eat sweets after school,

2 Jim swims twice a week now that he has a new job,

3 Katie used to go to bed at midnight every night,

4 Ahmed used to jog every Saturday morning,

5 Maria stretches her muscles for ten minutes before she runs,

6 People used to think that exercise was only for young people,

a but now she goes to bed much earlier.

b but she used to put on her running shoes and just go!

c but now he plays soccer with his friends.

d but now I eat fresh fruit such as apples and oranges.

e but now they know that exercise is something you do all your life.

f but he used to swim every day.

C **Circle the best answer for each sentence.**

1 Maggie and her friends **ran** / **used to run** ten kilometers yesterday morning.

2 Dan's grandfather **swam** / **used to swim** in this lake when he was a boy.

3 Last night, Anna's family **had** / **used to have** vegetables with their dinner.

4 The students **drank** / **used to drink** a lot of juice at yesterday's party.

5 Victor **watched** / **used to watch** television at night, but now he rides his bicycle.

6 Maki **thought** / **used to think** you were going to exercise with her last night.

D Complete the sentence pairs using the verbs in the box. One sentence in each pair uses a verb with *used to*. One sentence uses the past tense of the verb.

get up	eat	wear	~~make~~

1 Our coach **made** us clean the locker room last night.

Our coach **used to make** us run every night after practice.

2 Stanley ____________ a large ice cream cone every day after school.

Stanley ____________ a large green salad after school today.

3 Jennifer ____________ her old tennis shoes when she went running.

Jennifer ____________ her new running shoes this morning.

4 Marcel ____________ at 7:30 this morning to exercise.

Marcel ____________ at 5:30 every morning to exercise.

E Unscramble the sentences.

1 eat / every / Sonia / to / day / used / apples / two

Sonia used to eat two apples every day.

2 weigh / kilograms / used / to / over / George / ninety

____

3 every / grandfather / walk / to / My / used / day / school / to

____

4 used / hiking / afternoon / go / Burak / to / Saturday / every

____

F Write one sentence about something you used to do but don't do anymore.

____

____

Student Book page 121

Communicate

Word Study

A **Complete the chart with the words in the box. Then number. You will not use every word.**

~~navigate~~ duplicate estimate concentrate exaggerate graduate
navigation duplication estimation concentration exaggeration graduation

	Noun	Verb
1	navigation	**navigate**
2		duplicate
3		estimate

	Noun	Verb
4	concentration	
5		exaggerate
6	graduation	

[ ] 

[ ] 

[ ] 

[ ] 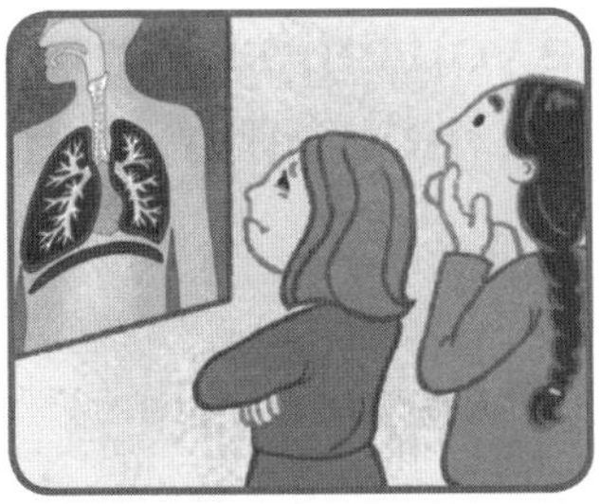

[ ] 

[1] 

B **Circle the correct words.**

Before our **graduate / graduation** (1) from wilderness camp, my friends and I had to **navigate / navigation** (2) our way through the forest back to our cabins. It wasn't easy. I **estimation / estimate** (3) that it took us about two hours of hiking to get back. During that time, we had to **concentrate / concentration** (4) on where we were, so we didn't get lost. It's not an **exaggerate / exaggeration** (5) to say it was the best experience of my life. It isn't a test that you could **duplication / duplicate** (6) anywhere else.

Writing Study

A **Complete the sentences with the verbs in the box. Use the correct verb form.**

have	work	want	jump	play	know	go	pump

1 Something in the body ______________ blood 24 hours a day. What is it?

2 Everybody ______________ that exercise is good for our bodies.

3 Nothing in the body ______________ harder than the heart.

4 Does anybody here ______________ to go swimming with me?

5 Everything in the body ______________ a job to do to keep us healthy.

6 Anything that you breathe in ______________ into your lungs.

7 In gym class, nobody ______________ as high as Neema.

8 Does somebody in the classroom ______________ tennis?

B **Read. Then write a paragraph about a kind of exercise you enjoy. Write at least one sentence with *used to*. Be sure to use sentences with indefinite pronouns that have subject / verb agreement.**

> I **used to** think that exercise was boring. Now I know it can be really fun. My favorite exercise is jumping rope. If **nobody is** around, you can jump alone. If **somebody wants** to join you, you can jump together. **Everyone has** fun jumping rope.

Wrap Up

Writing

A Read this interview with a body part. Label the parts of the report.

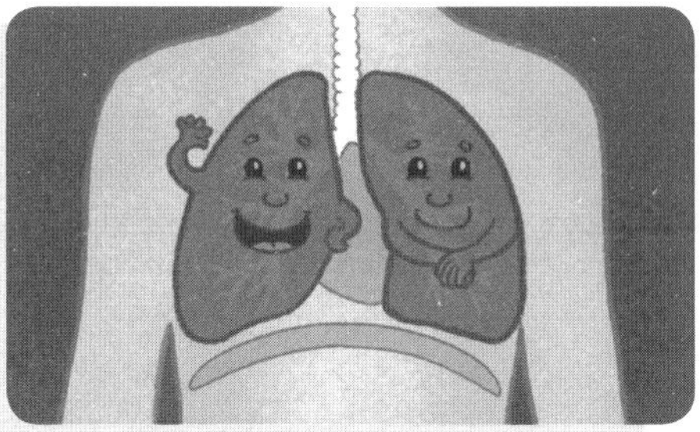

An Interview with the Human Lungs

Amy: My guests today are two twins called the lungs. How are you today?

Lungs: We're doing great, Amy.

Amy: You both have an important job to do, right?

Right Lung: That's right. We bring in oxygen from outside of the body.

Left Lung: Then we transfer that oxygen to the blood so that the heart can send it out to the whole body. We also get rid of the carbon dioxide that our body produces.

Amy: Wow! You must be busy.

Right Lung: Yes, we're very busy. We breathe in and out about 20,000 times a day.

Amy: Where are you located in the body?

Right Lung: I'm on the right side of the chest, and my twin is on the left side.

Amy: Do any other body parts help you with your job?

Left Lung: Our friend the diaphragm helps us to expand and shrink so that we can inhale and exhale air easily.

Amy: Well, thanks for taking time to talk to me today. I really enjoyed it!

Right Lung: Amy, talking to you was a breath of fresh air for us.

B Plan your interview. Brainstorm interesting questions and find answers for your interview. Write them in the chart below.

The Body Part I Will Interview: ______________________

Questions	Answers

C Now go to your notebook to write your own interview with a body part of your choice.

My writing checklist:

- ☐ I wrote my interview as if I were really talking with someone.
- ☐ I chose the most interesting questions for my interview.
- ☐ I did research to find the correct answers to these questions.
- ☐ I included an interesting title.

What did you learn?

____

____

____

____

____

____

____

____

____

____

____

____

____

____

____

____

____

____

____

____

____

BIG QUESTION 6

How do our bodies work?

Review

A **Look at the pictures. Complete the sentences with the words in the box.**

inhale virus exhale swallow common cold mucus

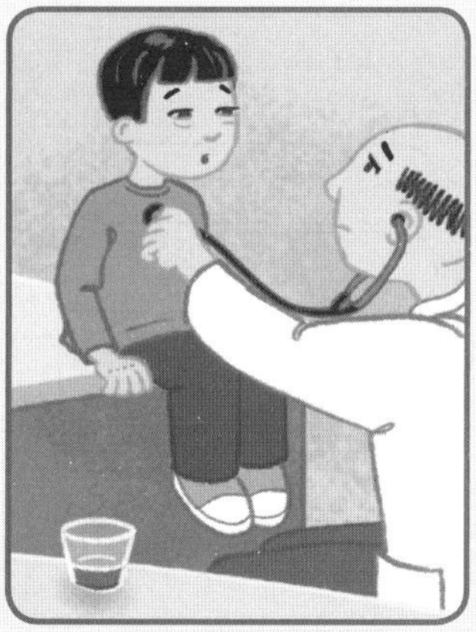

This young boy has a ________ (1). It is caused by a ________ (2). The boy has ________ (3) in his nose and throat. To check the boy's lungs, the doctor asks him to ________ (4) and ________ (5). The boy will need to ________ (6) some medicine.

lungs pumping trachea pulse concentrating heart

This girl is in a race. As she breathes quickly, air goes through her ________ (7) and into her ________ (8). She is checking her ________ (9) with her fingers to see how fast her ________ (10) is ________ (11). She is ________ (12) on winning the race.

B **Circle the correct words. Then write the adjectives in the correct order.**

Does anybody **knows** / **know** what this ______________ (green, triangular, small) object is under this microscope? I think it's a plant cell, but nobody in my group **is** / **are** sure. I hope it's not a ______________ (new, dangerous) virus. Hopefully our ______________ (young, talented) science teacher can tell me what it is.

C **Complete the sentence pairs using the verbs in the box. One sentence in each pair uses a verb with *used to*. One sentence uses the past tense of the verb.**

do	exercise	bake	dream

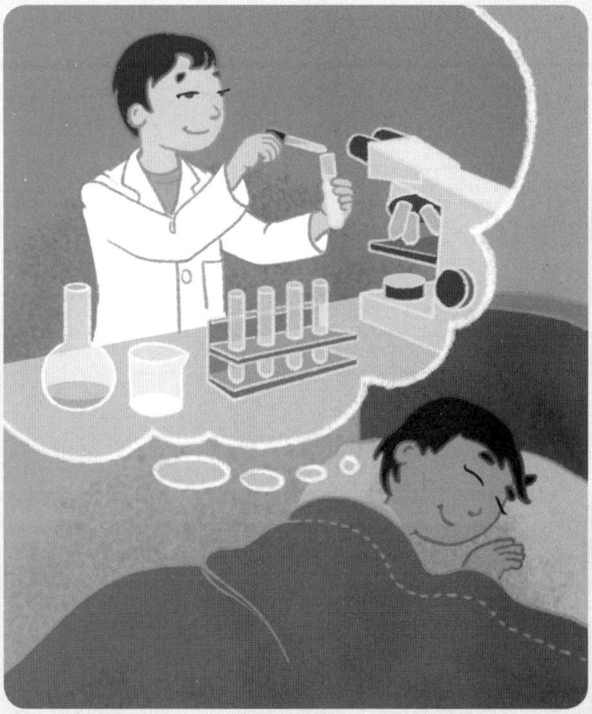

1 When I was a boy, I ______________ that I was a famous soccer player.

Last night in bed, I ______________ that I was a famous scientist.

2 My gym coach ______________ one hundred push-ups yesterday.

My gym coach ______________ two hundred push-ups when he was younger.

3 My mother ______________ chocolate chip cookies every Saturday afternoon.

Last Saturday afternoon, my mother ______________ healthy banana muffins.

4 Marisa ______________ for thirty minutes after school today.

Marisa ______________ for one hour every day after school.

D **Write commands to your friends and family about their health.**

1 Don't eat so many sweets. Eat healthy food such as fruit and nuts.

2 ______________________________

3 ______________________________

BIG QUESTION 7

What is the mass media?

Think and write.

What do you know?

____

____

____

____

____

____

____

____

____

What do you want to know?

____

____

____

____

____

____

____

____

____

UNIT 13 Get Ready

Words

A Look and write.

printing press	smartphone	advertising	blog
publisher	newspaper	magazine	broadcast

1

____

2
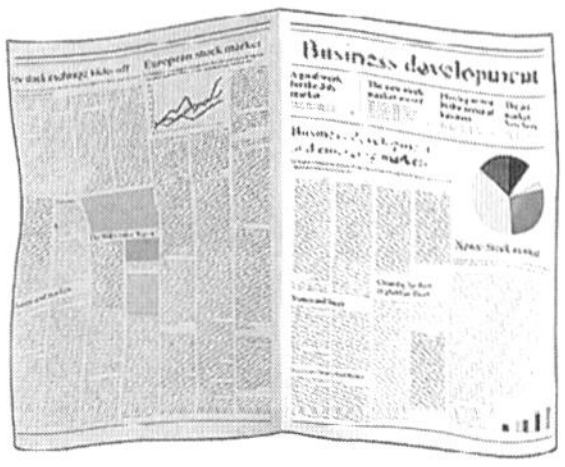

____

3

____

4
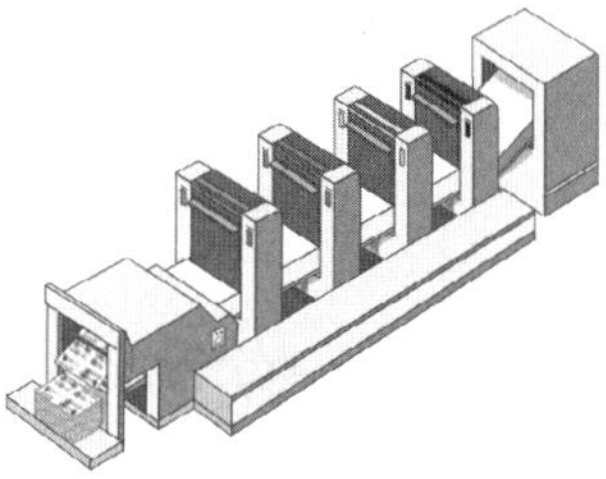

____

5

____

6

____

7

____

8
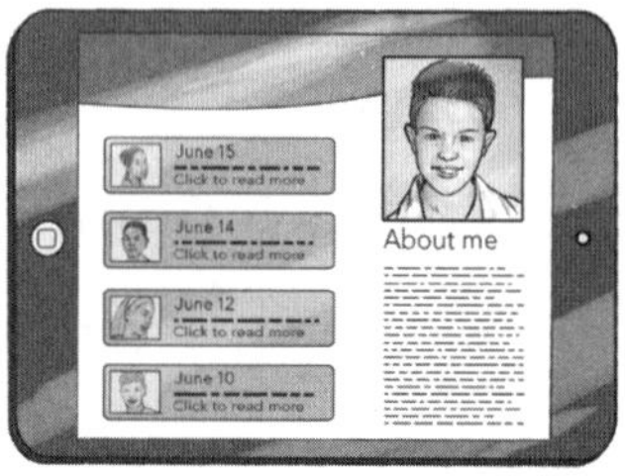

____

Student Book pages 126–128

B Unscramble and write.

The __________ is a powerful communication tool. This form of __________
1 bwe 2 sasm imade
can __________ news and information almost instantly around the world. In
3 radabtosc
addition, people can share information through __________ and __________.
4 solgb 5 locais rekwsont

C Circle the correct words.

1 Tara was very excited to get a **smartphone** / **printing press** for her birthday.

2 Laurent is proud to have his own **social network** / **blog** that he writes every day.

3 Malin's favorite **newspaper** / **magazine** is all about tennis.

4 The **mass media** / **printing press** includes radio and television, too.

5 The **Web** / **publisher** of this newspaper sells over one million copies a day.

6 Social networks often **broadcast** / **advertising** news faster than newspapers.

D Complete the sentences with the word pairs in the box.

blogs–social networks	advertising–magazines	publishers–printing presses
Web–mass media	newspaper–smartphone	

1 The __________ is one of the fastest forms of __________.

2 I like the creative __________ in some fashion __________.

3 I used to read the __________ for news. Now I use my __________.

4 Newspaper __________ need fast __________ to get the news out.

5 I spend my free time reading __________ and chatting on __________.

A Read the news story. Why did the news about the fire travel so fast?

____

____

B Read the news story again. As you read, think about the main ideas and the details that support them.

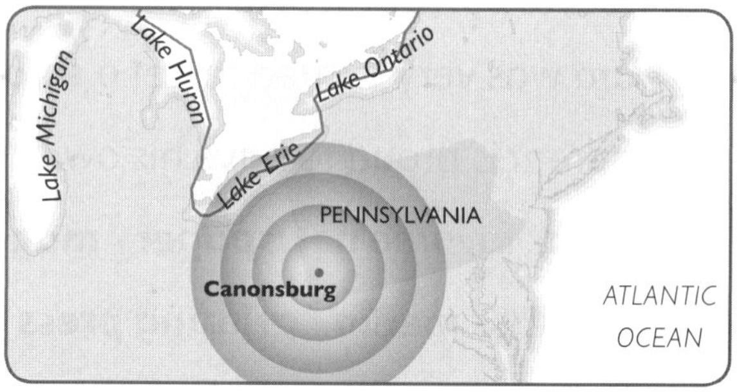

News Travels Fast

The Sarris Candy Company is a family-owned company in Canonsburg, Pennsylvania. They make delicious chocolates and candies and sell them to people all over the world. On February 3, 2012, a fire started at the company. News about the fire traveled very quickly.

At 7:00 a.m., workers at the company smelled smoke. They heard a fire alarm and had to leave the building immediately. Very soon, many fire engines arrived.

News traveled quickly in Canonsburg. First, the workers called their families. Then, neighbors and friends spread the news through phone calls, text messages, and e-mails. One worker received twenty messages on his **smartphone**. His friends asked if he was okay. Fortunately, no one was hurt.

Think
What is the main idea in this paragraph? What details support it?

Firefighters worked hard to put out the fire. Then local television and **newspaper** people came. They took photographs and videos. They also talked to some of the company's workers. By noon, news about the fire was on televisions everywhere in Pennsylvania. Many people in their cars heard the news on their radios.

That afternoon, **printing presses** in many cities printed the evening newspapers. The newspapers had detailed stories about the fire. Major television stations also **broadcast** the news. The **Web** had information about the fire, too. By that night, many people around the United States knew what happened at the Sarris Candy Company.

Four days later, the company posted a message on some **social networks** on the Web. They thanked their customers everywhere for their kind words after the fire.

Think
What is the main idea in this paragraph? What details support it?

On March 1, 2012, the company opened again. Today, it continues to make all the delicious chocolates and sweets that people know and love.

Comprehension

A What did the news story teach you about the mass media and communication? Write two things you learned.

____

____

B Write the number of each supporting detail under its main idea.

~~1~~ Local television and newspaper people came to report on the fire.

2 Neighbors and friends spread the news.

3 The workers at the company called their families.

4 Printing presses in many cities printed the evening newspapers.

5 The Web had information about the fire.

6 Many people in their cars heard the news on their radios.

People in Canonsburg heard the news.	People in Pennsylvania heard the news.	People around the United States heard the news.
	1	

C Answer the questions.

1 How did the workers at the company first know about the fire?

____

2 Who spread the news about the fire in the town of Canonsburg?

____

3 How did people around the United States know about the fire?

____

D **Words in Context** Read and write.

journalist	newsreels	radio station	latest

1 My uncle works at a ______________. You can hear him every morning at 8:00.

2 Ken watches the news every night at 10:00 to get the ______________ information.

3 The students watched ______________ from the 1920s in history class.

4 Manuel is a ______________ who has to travel to report on news when it happens.

Grammar in Use

A Study the grammar.

Learn ***Must, Mustn't, Have To, Don't Have To***

Reggie	**must watch** / **mustn't watch**	television after school.
Daria	**has to use** / **doesn't have to use**	the Web for her homework.
The radio stations	**have to broadcast** / **don't have to broadcast**	the news.
Workers at the company	**had to leave** / **didn't have to leave**	the building.

B Complete the sentences with the words in the box.

have to don't have to has to doesn't have to had to didn't have to mustn't

1 Information in newspapers __________ be correct at all times.

2 You ____________________ own a smartphone, but it's very useful.

3 Lisa ____________________ write a comment on my blog, but I'm happy she did.

4 Students ____________________ chat on social networks while they are at school.

5 My father ____________________ deliver newspapers when he was a boy.

6 Most publishers ____________________ include advertising in their newspapers.

7 A blog ____________________ look fancy. It just needs interesting news.

C Circle the correct words.

1 People **don't have to** / **mustn't** use the Web to get important news.

2 Students **must** / **mustn't** use their smartphones in class.

3 You **mustn't** / **don't have to** join a social network on the Web.

4 Jon **doesn't have to** / **has to** buy a daily newspaper, but he always does.

D Rewrite the sentences to make them correct.

1 Students ~~must~~ mustn't bring their smartphones into the classroom with them.

Students mustn't bring their smartphones into the classroom with them.

2 The students don't have to read newspaper articles in English class.

____

____

3 People who use social networks have to share news on the phone.

____

____

4 Pam's television isn't working, so she doesn't have to use the radio to get the news.

____

____

E Unscramble the sentences.

1 printing / has / The / new / press / a / publisher / buy / to

____

2 have / to / blog / advertising / doesn't / have / A

____

3 network / have / join / People / social / to / a / don't

____

4 news / must / mass / important / broadcast / The / media

____

5 don't / play / use / have / games / the / to / You / Web / to

____

Word Study

knowledge	knot	knight	knit	kneel	knuckle

A **Look and write. Circle each *silent k* word.**

1

____

2

____

3

____

4

____

5

____

6

____

B **Complete the sentences with words from the box.**

1 This new novel is about a brave ______________ who serves his queen.

2 Pam hurt her ______________ while she was playing volleyball yesterday.

3 It is important to have ______________, but you must also learn how to use it.

4 Please don't ______________ on the grass in your white pants. They will get dirty.

5 Philip's brother works on a sailboat, and he can tie almost any kind of ______________.

6 Tina's grandmother likes to ______________ sweaters for her grandchildren.

Writing Study

A **Replace the underlined nouns with the correct pronouns.**

- My father likes to read the newspaper. In fact, ~~my father~~ (1) **he** reads the newspaper (2) from front to back every morning before work.

- The printing press was broken, so people came to fix the printing press (3). However, the people (4) couldn't fix the printing press (5) because they didn't have the right parts.

Soon, the people (6) got the right parts (7), and the people (8) fixed the printing press very quickly.

B **Write a paragraph about how news travels. Write at least one sentence using *must* or *have to*. Be sure to use pronouns that match your nouns.**

A boy at our school broke his leg. Soon, all of his classmates knew about his leg. **He had to** go to the hospital to get a cast on **it**. The school nurse called his parents, and **they** went to see **him**. The next week, there was a story about **him** in the school newspaper.

Get Ready

Words

A Find and circle.

h	s	s	u	c	s	i	d	h	s	i	s
r	n	e	o	s	c	o	i	u	s	n	w
m	h	r	m	e	f	w	n	e	t	v	h
d	e	c	i	d	e	p	s	a	i	e	r
h	a	l	s	w	h	c	r	a	e	s	e
n	d	e	t	i	s	b	e	w	v	t	p
o	l	e	a	b	t	s	a	v	n	i	o
e	i	p	k	z	o	c	r	n	e	g	r
i	n	t	e	r	v	i	e	w	h	a	t
f	e	v	a	t	a	s	e	h	d	t	e
r	n	c	e	e	r	o	t	i	d	e	r
i	a	h	e	r	o	h	c	a	r	e	s

investigate
editor
decide
reporter
search
hero
discuss
website
interview
mistake
headline

B Look and number.

1 reporter **2** headline **3** search **4** interview **5** hero **6** website

☐ 

☐ 

☐ 

☐ 

☐ 

☐ 

investigate	editor	decide	reporter	search	hero
discuss	website	interview	mistake	headline	

C **Write the words in the correct boxes.**

People	Actions	Things

D **Complete the sentences with the words in the box.**

1 There's a great ________________ on the Web that reports the news for children.

2 My family and I often ________________ the news when we're eating dinner.

3 A ________________ from the local television station came to our art exhibition.

4 It's quite easy to ________________ for information on the Web.

5 Our English teacher is the ________________ of the school newspaper.

6 My sister can't ________________ if she wants to work in television or radio.

7 The reporter asked his guest some good questions during the ________________ .

8 Bobby is a ________________ for saving those kittens from the burning barn.

9 Arnold will ________________ the facts before he writes about the story.

10 Every ________________ in today's newspapers was about the factory fire.

11 The magazine article made a ________________ about the actor's age.

A Read. What clues help Jack solve the case?

B Read again. What is the conflict? What possible resolutions are there? What is the final resolution to the conflict?

Jack Jackson, Reporter

Jack Jackson was a normal boy who liked playing baseball with his friends. Not many people knew that his big brother was Ernie Jackson, the famous **reporter** for the *Calgary Times*.

One Saturday, Ernie told Jack that he was **investigating** a very difficult case and that he was worried he couldn't solve it. The case was about Madeline Mulrooney, the richest woman in Calgary. Her diamond ring was missing.

"She thinks her swimming coach took it," Ernie said. "However, he says he hasn't stolen anything. I'm not sure who to believe."

"I'll help you," said Jack. "Let's **interview** Mrs. Mulrooney together."

Think What's the main conflict in the story?

The brothers went to the Mulrooney mansion. Mrs. Mulrooney explained what happened. She said that she always put her ring on the coffee table before she swam in her pool.

"The water in the pool isn't good for my ring, and it also dries my skin," she said. "I always put on hand cream and wear cotton gloves to bed."

"Where are the gloves now?" Jack asked.

"I throw them away each morning," she said, pointing to a garbage can.

Jack rushed over to the can. He **searched** through it and pulled out many gloves. Carefully, he felt each one, and then he smiled.

Think What possible resolutions are there to the conflict?

"Your ring is right here," said Jack. "The cream was slippery, so your ring came off with this glove. You only noticed after swimming."

"You solved the case!" shouted Ernie.

"You're my **hero**!" said Mrs. Mulrooney.

The next day, the **headline** of the *Calgary Times* read, "Young Reporter Discovers Missing Diamond!" Jack celebrated by playing baseball with his friends. However, he wondered if there were any more cases to solve.

Understand

Comprehension

A Would you like to be a reporter? Write why or why not.

____

____

B Complete the chart with information about "Jack Jackson, Reporter."

Conflict	Possible Resolutions	Actual Resolution
Madeline Mulrooney's diamond ring is missing.		

C Answer the questions.

1 What is Jack's brother's job?

____

2 Why does Mrs. Mulrooney take her ring off while she swims?

____

3 What does Mrs. Mulrooney do with the cotton gloves after she uses them?

____

4 How did the ring come off Mrs. Mulrooney's finger?

____

D **Words in Context** Read and write.

mansion	terrible	donated	fair

1 It was a ____________ day for Mrs. Mulrooney when she lost her ring.

2 It wasn't ____________ of Mrs. Mulrooney to think that the coach took her ring.

3 Jack was not surprised that Mrs. Mulrooney lived in a ____________ .

4 Mrs. Mulrooney gave Jack some money, but he ____________ it to a hospital.

Student Book page 140

Grammar in Use

A Study the grammar.

Learn **Present Perfect**

She **has checked** / **hasn't checked** this article for mistakes.

They **have investigated** / **haven't investigated** the story.

The swimming coach **has stolen** something. / **hasn't stolen** anything.

We **have written** / **haven't written** a blog.

Irregular Verbs		
Present	**Past**	**Past Participle**
steal	stole	stolen
write	wrote	written

B **Complete the sentences with *has, have, hasn't,* or *haven't.* Change the verb to the correct tense.**

1 Ala has found (find) a new website that reports the latest sports news from around the world. She reads it two or three times a day.

2 Bill's editor ____________ (finish) checking his news story. Now it can be printed in tonight's newspaper.

3 Students ____________ (decide) what to call their new school newspaper. They may call it *The Student Gazette, The Student Post,* or something else.

4 The journalists ____________ (interview) the mayor about the new city park. Everyone will hear about it on the local television news tonight.

5 The company president ____________ (discuss) her plans with any reporters. She will hold a news conference when she has more information.

C Match.

1 The students in our class have •   • **a** made any mistakes in his newspaper.

2 The editor of the *Gazette* hasn't •   • **b** met each other many times before.

3 This printing press hasn't •   • **c** worked hard on the class newspaper.

4 The writer and editor have •   • **d** stopped printing all day.

D Unscramble the sentences.

1 reporter / for / The / information / searched / has

____

2 the / changed / editor / headline / The / has

____

3 publisher / has / Amber / worked / a / for

____

4 program / awards / news / many / won / has / The

____

5 for / taken / photographer / has / magazines / The / pictures

____

E Write present perfect sentences.

1 the reporter / not write / the story

The reporter hasn't written the story.

2 Eduardo / not listen / to the news on the radio

____

3 As an interviewer, / Angela / speak / to some important people

____

4 Fiona / not watch / a newsreel, but her grandmother has

____

5 Pedro / travel / for his blog

____

F Write one sentence about something that you have done.

____

Communicate

Word Study

huge   entire   special   whole   immense   unusual

A **Read and match. Circle the words that are synonyms. Then number.**

1 My father's entire family watched Neil Armstrong step onto the moon on July 21, 1969.

2 There was a special report in the newspaper today. It was about the number of organic supermarkets in our city.

3 The Web is huge, and it continues to grow every day.

a There is an immense number of websites on it. It would be impossible to see them all.

b He says the whole world was watching it on television or listening to it on the radio.

c The report said that it was unusual for a city of our size to have so many of them.

☐ 

☐ 

☐ 

B **Circle the correct words.**

1 A(n) **special** / **entire** page in the newspaper was about the stolen paintings.

2 The television station has a **whole** / **special** reporter who investigates cases.

3 There is a(n) **immense** / **whole** radio tower in our town that you can see from far away.

4 The editor made a mistake yesterday, and it's **huge** / **unusual** for her to do that.

5 A(n) **huge** / **entire** story about the Olympic games took up ten pages of the magazine.

6 The students spent a **whole** / **immense** class period discussing the mass media.

Writing Study

A **Complete the sentences with the verbs in the box. Use the present perfect form. Write *R* for regular verbs and *I* for irregular verbs.**

start	~~make~~	fly	buy	search	turn	bring	answer

1 The writer of this newspaper article has __made__ too many mistakes. __I__

2 This television report about our city has __________ all my questions. _____

3 Nadia has __________ to Europe to report on the ice skating event. _____

4 The police have __________ everywhere for the missing painting. _____

5 Missy has __________ a blog about keeping our planet healthy. _____

6 The Web has __________ us information from around the world. _____

7 We've __________ ingredients to make a healthy dinner. _____

8 Everybody has __________ off their smartphones before the concert. _____

B **Read. Then write a paragraph about a job you would like to do in the mass media. Use present perfect sentences with the correct form of the verb. Write at least one sentence using regular verbs and one sentence using irregular verbs.**

I **haven't been** a reporter, but I would like to be one. **I've read** many news articles in newspapers and magazines, so I understand the writing style. **I've** also **traveled** to many places, and **I've taken** many photographs with my camera.

____

____

____

____

____

____

Wrap Up

Writing

A Read this news story about a real event. Label the parts of the story.

Local Girl Wins Area Spelling Bee

by Thomas Porter

Mia Silva, a 4th-grade student at Central Elementary School here in Redwood, is the new spelling bee champion in the area.

Last night, at exactly 7:35 p.m., Mia Silva stood on stage at the Jane Austen Arena. Her parents were watching nervously. Mia took a breath, and then she listened to the speaker say the final word of the spelling competition.

"The word was *troubadour*," Mia said later. "It's a European musician from long ago. I knew the word started out like *trouble*, and then it was easy to remember the rest of it."

Mia spelled the word correctly. She has now become the top speller among students from fifty elementary schools. Next week, she will go to the national competition.

Mia says she isn't too worried. Her mother agrees. "Mia hasn't been nervous," she said. "She just enjoys everything she does. She loves reading, writing, and being with friends."

The town of Redwood congratulates Mia for doing so well. Mia, best of luck as you go on to the national competition!

B Plan your news story about a real event. Use the chart below to organize your ideas.

Who	
What	
When	
Where	
Why	
Quotes	

C Now go to your notebook to write your own news story about a real event.

My writing checklist:

- ☐ My news story answered *who*, *what*, *when*, *where*, and *why*.
- ☐ My news story had a headline and a byline.
- ☐ My news story included a lead to catch the reader's attention.
- ☐ My news story included information and quotes from an interview.
- ☐ All the information in my news story was correct.

Student Book page 144

What did you learn?

BIG QUESTION 7

What is the mass media?

Review

A Complete the puzzle.

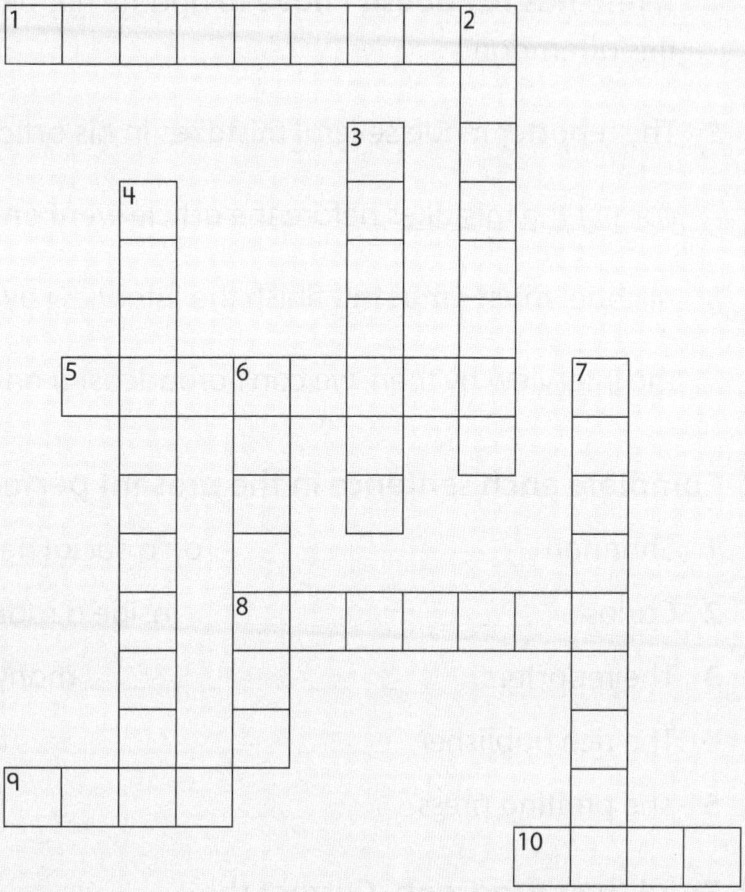

Across →

1 This person or company prints and sells things we read.

5 You will find this at the top of an article.

8 Not common or normal

9 Very large

10 This person has done something brave to help others.

Down ↓

2 This person gets news and tells us about it through the media.

3 This is a large house.

4 This makes us want to buy or do something.

6 To talk about something with someone

7 We get this when we go to school.

knowledge	hero	unusual	mansion
advertising	huge	headline	
reporter	magazine	publisher	

B Circle the correct words. Replace the underlined nouns with pronouns.

1 Teresa **has to / doesn't have to** update her blog tonight. Teresa worked on her blog this afternoon.

2 The reporter made several mistakes in his article. The reporter **had to / didn't have to** correct the mistakes before the article went on the Web.

3 Michael **must / mustn't** finish the interview by 4:00 p.m. If Michael doesn't finish the interview by then, we can't broadcast it on the evening news.

C Complete each sentence in the present perfect. Use the verbs in parentheses.

1 Shannon ________________ on a social network. (not chat)

2 Carlos ____________________ inside a radio station. (not be)

3 The reporters ____________________ many cases in our city. (investigate)

4 The rich publisher ____________________ to donate his mansion to the city. (decide)

5 The printing press ____________________ this morning's newspapers. (not print)

D Read the paragraph. Correct the underlined words.

I have enjoy being a sports reporter for my school newspaper. I have meet lots of people, and sometimes I have interview him. I also don't have to take pictures at sports events. Last night, I went to a basketball game. I hasn't played basketball, and it looked difficult! I took pictures and put it on the school website. Today I mustn't write an article about the game. I'm in a hurry, because we has to print the newspaper by Friday afternoon.

BIG QUESTION 8

What can we learn from nature's power?

Think and write.

What do you know?

What do you want to know?

Student Book pages 146–148

Words

rescue worker collapse tsunami blizzard
power lines thunderstorm tornado
earthquake victim flood hurricane

A Look and write.

1 

2 

3 

4 

5 

B Write the words.

1
2
3
4
5
6

C Match.

1 During our soccer game, the ground began to move back and forth.

2 I heard yesterday that a tsunami reached the coast of China.

3 Last night a big thunderstorm went through Harold's town.

4 This spring the North River rose too high.

a The wave pushed a large amount of water onto the land, but no one was hurt.

b He couldn't sleep because the lightning in the sky was so bright. The storm also made a lot of noise.

c It caused a flood in the American town of Springfield.

d It was an earthquake! It was difficult to stand, so we all sat down on the field.

e

f

g

h

D Complete the sentences with word pairs from the box.

power lines–collapsed	rescue workers–victims	tornado–blizzard

1 After the hurricane, the ____________________ gave food and clothing to the ____________________ who lost their homes in the storm.

2 The storm last night was too strong for some ____________________ in our city. Some of them ____________________.

3 Although they are both very dangerous, a ____________________ is more powerful than a ____________________.

A Read the article. How does time save lives?

B Read the article again. As you read about each warning system, ask yourself, *what are the causes* and *what are the effects?*

Early Warning Systems

Have you ever heard a loud siren in your city? It is part of an early warning system. These systems give people time to protect themselves against different, dangerous forces of nature.

Earthquake Warning Systems

An **earthquake** can happen at any time. Some countries now have earthquake sensors. Scientists have put them in many places. When a sensor feels the ground move, it sends a signal to warn people that an earthquake will happen soon. Some signals go to moving trains so that they can stop. Other signals go to smartphones. After the signal, people have up to twenty seconds to get to a safe place and protect themselves before they feel the earthquake.

Tsunami Warning Systems

Think
What causes a sensor to send a signal? What effects happen after it sends the signal?

Scientists have put floating buoys on the ocean. They measure waves and water pressure. If a **tsunami** moves under them, the buoys send signals to scientists. The scientists then alert a country's government, and the government broadcasts a warning to people along the coast. People hear the warning through televisions, radios, smartphones, and sirens. They then have time to leave quickly and stay safe. Tsunamis can destroy whole cities on the coast, so this warning system is very important.

Hurricane Warning Systems

Think
What causes the buoys to send signals? What effects happen after they send the signals?

Scientists watch **hurricanes** grow from cameras in space. Planes and ships go near hurricanes to get information. When scientists think a hurricane might reach land, they issue a hurricane *watch*. This is broadcast through radio and television. People then prepare for it. When scientists know a hurricane will reach land soon, they issue a *warning* and people leave the area.

There are early warning systems for **tornados**, **thunderstorms**, **blizzards**, and **floods**, too. People receive information and act quickly. As a result, there are fewer **victims** of these forces of nature.

Student Book page 149

Understand

Comprehension

A Have you ever experienced a force of nature? Write what happened.

____

____

B Match each cause with two effects.

Cause	First Effect	Second Effect
1 An earthquake happens.	a It passes under buoys on the ocean. The buoys send signals.	d People receive this *watch* or *warning* on radios and televisions.
2 A tsunami is coming toward the coast.	b If it is not close, the government issues a *watch*. If it is close, they issue a *warning*.	e Moving trains get the signal. People with smartphones get the signal.
3 A hurricane is moving toward land.	c The ground moves under a sensor. It sends a signal.	f A warning reaches people on radios, televisions, sirens, and smartphones.

C Answer the questions.

1 What do floating buoys on the ocean measure?

____

2 What do people do when they receive a hurricane warning?

____

D **Words in Context** Read and write.

forces	funnel	horizontally	vertically

1 A tornado spins ______________ from the sky to the ground.

2 A tsunami is one of the most dangerous ______________ of nature.

3 Hurricanes can be ______________ wider than a country.

4 Most tornadoes are shaped like a giant ______________ .

Student Book page 152

Grammar in Use

A Study the grammar.

Learn **Present Perfect with *Ever* and *Never***

Questions	Answers
Have you / they ***ever* heard** a loud siren?	Yes, I / they **have**. / No, I / they **haven't**.
	I'**ve** / They'**ve** ***never* heard** one.
Has she / he ***ever* been** in a storm?	Yes, she / he **has**. / No, she / he **hasn't**.
	She'**s** / He'**s** ***never* been** in a storm.

B **Cross out the underlined mistake. Write the correct word above it. Then answer the question.**

Has
1 ~~Have~~ Patrick ever prepared for a hurricane?
Yes, he has.

2 Have you ever hear the sound of a tornado?
No, ______________ .

3 Have buildings never collapsed in this city? ______, ______ haven't.

4 Has Maria ever thank the rescue workers? Yes, ______________ .

5 Has they ever slept through a thunderstorm? No, ______________ .

6 Have hurricane ever gone through this area? Yes, ______________ .

7 Has a tsunami never reached the coast of Hawaii? ______, ______ has.

8 Has these rivers ever caused a flood? No, ______________ .

9 Have these buoys ever sank to the bottom? ______, ______ haven't.

10 Has you ever been a victim of a hurricane?
Yes, ______________ .

11 Did they ever walked home in a blizzard?
No, ______________ .

C Circle the correct word. Then write *ever* in the correct position in the sentence.

1 **Have** / **Has** anyone ever survived outside in a blizzard?

2 Have earthquakes **happened** / **happen** in Greenland?

3 **Has** / **Have** those power lines collapsed during a hurricane?

4 Have rescue workers in this city **help** / **helped** you?

D Unscramble the sentences. Then match.

1 flood / been / Have / a / ever / you / in

____

____

2 tower / this / lightning / Has / ever / struck

____

____

3 systems / warning / ever / Have / failed / early

____

____

☐ No, they haven't. ☐ Yes, I have. ☐ Yes, it has.

E Read. Then answer each question. Use *never* when necessary.

1 Has Tom ever been in a flood? (✗)

No, Tom has never been in a flood.

2 Have hurricanes ever occurred in tropical areas? (✓)

____

3 Has Kelly ever felt an earthquake? (✗)

____

4 Have they ever experienced a blizzard? (✗)

____

Communicate

Word Study

snowfall	haircut	teamwork	raindrop	landslide	bodyguard

A **Circle the noun and underline the verb in each compound noun. Then match.**

1 During the storm, some of the raindrops that fell were the size of small oval coins.

2 The singer's car got stuck in a blizzard, but her bodyguards pushed it out of the snow.

3 When the ground started to shake yesterday, my barber was giving me a haircut.

4 The landslide happened during the hurricane, but luckily only a small shed was destroyed.

5 We had a large snowfall in our town last night, so the school was closed today.

6 Thanks to some great teamwork, the students were able to quickly clean up the beach after the hurricane.

a

b

c

d

e

f

B **Complete the sentences with the words in the box.**

1 The ________________ during the blizzard was over one meter deep.

2 The hurricane loosened the ground on the mountain and caused a ________________ .

3 The citizens showed ________________ by cleaning the streets after the thunderstorm.

4 The president's ________________ helped him get under a table during the earthquake.

5 The blizzard blocked the roads, so Pam couldn't get a ________________ at the salon.

6 There was not one ________________ from the sky before the tornado appeared.

Writing Study

A **Rewrite the sentences using short forms.**

1 They have experienced many earthquakes in their country.

They've experienced many earthquakes in their country.

2 I have never been in a hurricane because I live far from the ocean.

3 She has met many rescue workers in her job.

4 The tsunami was powerful. It has damaged many coastal towns.

5 We have cleaned up the area where the power lines collapsed.

B **Read. Then write a paragraph about a force of nature that you have experienced. Write at least one present perfect question with *ever*. Be sure to use short forms in your present perfect sentences.**

Have you ever been in a blizzard? I live in central Canada, and we have lots of them. **I've** shoveled up to one meter of snow to get from our house to our car. My dad has driven in blizzards, too. However, **he's** never been stuck in the snow.

UNIT 16 Get Ready

Words

A **Read and write.**

bottled water storm shelter sleeping bag storm shutters first-aid kit
canned food supplies cash batteries flashlight emergency

1 In case of a(n) ______________________, you may need these.

2 ______________________

3 ______________________

4 ______________________

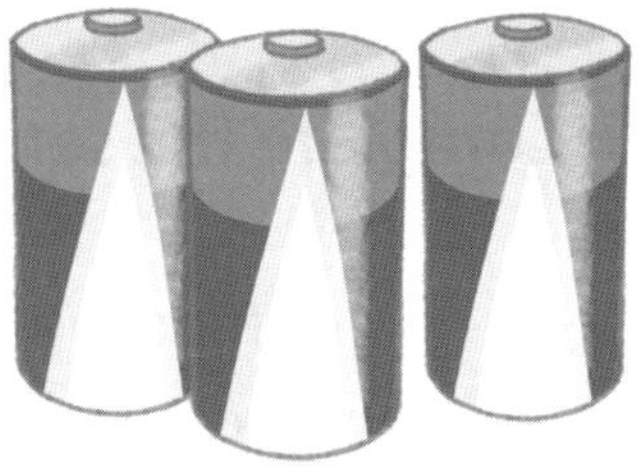

5 ______________________

6 ______________________

7 ______________________

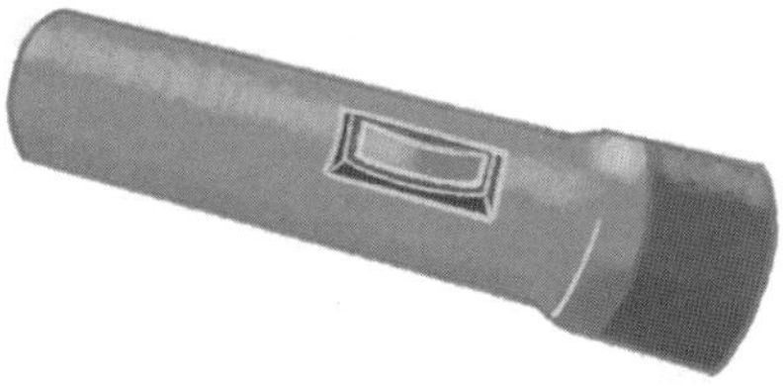

8 ______________________

9 ______________________

10 ______________________

11 ______________________

B Match each clue to a word.

1	You may need an opener to use this.	**a**	sleeping bag
2	This is important if you have a cut or a scratch.	**b**	cash
3	This can keep you warm if you spend the night outside.	**c**	storm shelter
4	This is useful if there is a store nearby.	**d**	canned food
5	You may meet other people here during a hurricane.	**e**	flashlight
6	This is very useful at night when there is no electricity in your house.	**f**	first-aid kit

C Circle True (T) or False (F).

1 Supplies can include food and blankets. T F

2 Batteries come in only one size. T F

3 Emergencies are often dangerous situations. T F

4 Storm shutters protect windows against hurricanes. T F

5 Bottled water can only be used for drinking. T F

D Complete the sentences with words from the box.

bottled water	storm shelter	sleeping bag	storm shutters	first-aid kit	
canned food	supplies	cash	batteries	flashlight	emergency

1 It's important to have enough ______________ during an ______________ so that you can buy the things you need.

2 Our house didn't have any ______________ for the windows, so we decided to stay at a ______________, where we were safer.

3 This ______________ doesn't shine very brightly. I think it needs new ______________.

4 We have enough ______________ to eat and ______________ to drink for five days.

5 We each have a ______________ to sleep in, a ______________ for cuts and scrapes, and ______________ for a few days.

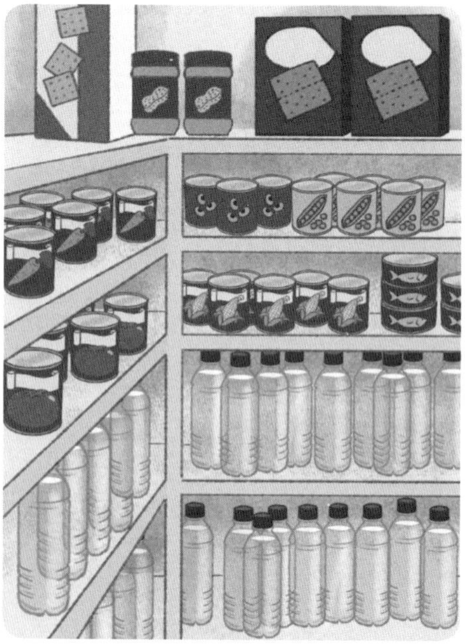

A **Read. Why is it important to know what to do in an emergency?**

B **Read again. As you read, remember to make inferences about the characters and events in the story.**

Working Together

It was 3:34 a.m. on February 27, 2010. Tomás Perez, his wife Sofia, and their three children were sleeping peacefully in their house in Concepción, Chile. Then, without warning, the house began to shake violently. Tomás woke up and immediately knew what to do.

"It's an earthquake! Move quickly!" he shouted. The children were already out of their beds, standing in the hallway. Their eyes were wide with surprise. The family ran downstairs to a large oak table in the kitchen. They hid under it and stayed close to each other. Sofia held Tamara, who was the youngest daughter. Tomás held the other children, Carla and her younger brother Matías. Books and dishes and glasses flew off the shelves and crashed to the ground. Pictures fell from the walls. Then, after three long, terrible minutes, the shaking stopped.

"Stay here," said Tomás. He walked carefully through all the rooms of the house. There was broken glass on the floor, but the house seemed okay. Tomás brought shoes for everyone. The earthquake cut off the electricity, so he also brought two **flashlights**.

> **Think**
> Make an inference. How did the family know where to go during the earthquake?

Carla began to sweep the floor. Tomás turned on a radio that used **batteries.** The reporter said that the earthquake was very large and very strong. Sofia brought blankets downstairs. She wrapped them around Tamara and Matías.

"We have enough **sleeping bags**, **canned food**, and **bottled water**," Tomás said. "However, our neighbors may need help. I haven't spoken to them yet. I will go see them now to make sure that they are safe. I will bring along this **first-aid kit**, too."

> **Think**
> Make an inference. Why is Tomás going to bring along a first-aid kit?

Many people lost their homes in the 2010 earthquake. However, the people of Chile worked together. They helped each other through this very difficult **emergency**.

Student Book page 158

Understand

Comprehension

A How do you think the characters felt in the reading? Would you have felt the same way? Why or why not?

____

____

B Read each inference. Match each inference to the correct person.

1 Tomás	**a** She is old enough to help her parents in an emergency.
2 Sofia	**b** They always work together and take care of each other.
3 Carla	**c** She cares a lot for her children.
4 Tamara and Matías	**d** He prepared his family well for an earthquake.
5 The Perez Family	**e** They are old enough to follow directions in an emergency.

C Circle True (T) or False (F).

1 The family hid under their beds during the earthquake. T F

2 The earthquake was three minutes long. T F

3 Tomás brought shoes because of the broken glass. T F

4 Tomás and his family needed more food and water. T F

D **Words in Context** Read and write.

inland destroyed trunk landfall

1 After the earthquake, a tsunami made ______________ along parts of the coast.

2 Many people in Chile moved ______________ to escape the tsunami.

3 The 2010 Chilean earthquake ______________ over 200,000 houses.

4 Some people keep emergency supplies in the ______________ of their car.

Grammar in Use

A Study the grammar.

Learn **Present Perfect with *Already*, *Just*, and *Yet***

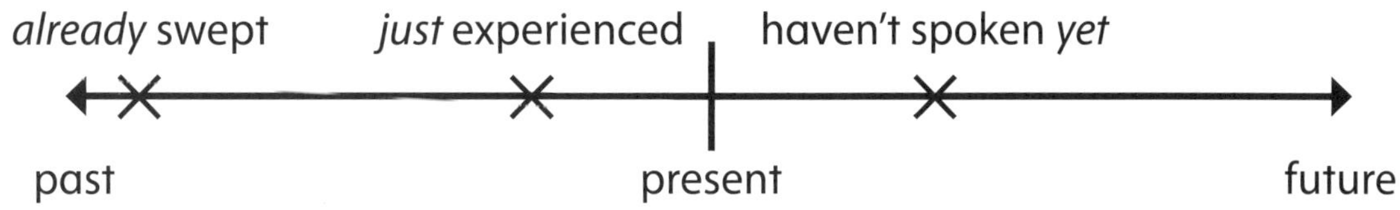

Statements	Questions
She **has *already* bought** extra bottled water.	**Has** she ***already* bought** extra bottled water?
We**'ve *just* experienced** an earthquake.	**Have** you ***just* experienced** an earthquake?
I **haven't spoken** to the neighbors ***yet***.	**Have** you **spoken** to the neighbors ***yet***?

B **Look at the circled X on the time chart at the end of each sentence. Rewrite the sentences with *already*, *just*, or *yet*.**

1 I've put the batteries in the flashlight.

I've just put the batteries in the flashlight.

2 He's returned from the storm shelter.

____

3 We haven't bought a new first-aid kit.

____

4 Have they washed the sleeping bags?

____

5 Has the canned food become too old?

____

6 Have you run out of supplies?

____

C Complete the sentences with *already*, *just*, or *yet*.

1 I've ______________ put emergency cash in the backpack. In fact, I did it two weeks ago.

2 He's ______________ put the storm shutters over all the windows. Now he's taking a break.

3 They haven't experienced a hurricane ______________ this year, but it's always possible during the season.

4 She's ______________ swept the floor in the kitchen. She still has the broom in her hand.

D Unscramble the sentences. Then match.

1 landfall / yet / tsunami / the / Has / made

____

2 canned / bought / We've / food / already

____

3 shelter / the / They've / storm / built / just

____

☐ 

☐ 

☐ 

E Imagine that you are preparing for an emergency. Write sentences using *already*, *just*, and *yet*.

1 I've already bought supplies.

2 ______________________________

3 ______________________________

4 ______________________________

Communicate

Word Study

turn down	turn over	turn on	turn in	turn up	turn back

A **Look. Then write the phrasal verbs from the box.**

1 

____

2 

____

3 

____

4 

____

5 

____

6 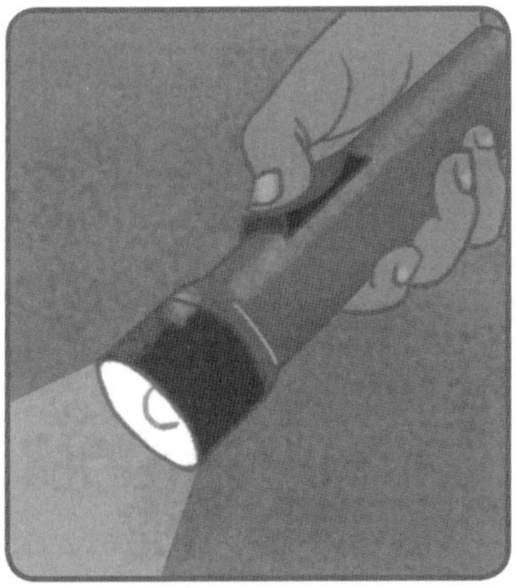

____

B **Complete the sentences with the phrasal verbs in the box. Use the correct tense.**

1 We have to ______________ and go home. The storm is too dangerous.

2 Put in the batteries and ______________ the radio. I want to hear the news report.

3 The students have ______________ their reports about hurricanes.

4 Please ______________ the heat. It's too cold inside the storm shelter.

5 Russell ______________ his sleeping bag and found his cash under it.

6 Could you ______________ the television? I'm listening to the storm outside.

Writing Study

A **Read the news story. Change the underlined adjectives to adverbs by adding *-ly*.**

A major hurricane has reached the city. The wind is

loudly

blowing ~~loud~~[1], and the waves are crashing violent[2] against the buildings near the beach. Fortunately, most people listened to the news careful[3] before the storm. They followed the emergency warning and are now sleeping quiet[4] in storm shelters. Some rescue workers are brave[5] searching for any victims. However, everyone seems to be safe, thanks to the government reporting the news accurate[6].

B **Read. Then write a paragraph that describes your family in an imaginary situation caused by a force of nature. Write at least one sentence in the present perfect using *already*, *just*, or *yet*. Use sentences with adverbs of manner that end in *-ly*.**

> **Has** the tornado **passed** us by **yet**? It is difficult to say. My family and I are waiting **bravely** in the basement of our house. The wind is blowing **loudly** outside. My little sister is sitting **quietly** on the sofa and reading a picture book.

Student Book page 163

Wrap Up

Writing

A Read this how-to speech about preparing for an emergency. Label the parts of the story.

Preparing for Floods

[ ] Hello, everyone!

[ ] Water gives us life. However, water can also be dangerous. For example, it's important to keep your family safe from floods. They may come quickly or slowly, but you must always be prepared for them. Here are some simple suggestions.

[ ] First, have emergency supplies ready at home, such as food, bottled water, and medicine. You should have enough for at least three days. Next, make a family plan so that you know where to go in case of a flood. If you are separated, you should plan where to meet.

[ ] In addition, if a flood is possible soon, listen to the radio or television. It's best to move immediately to higher ground if you don't know what to do. If you have time, you should take your important things to the highest place in your house. Finally, do not move around during a flood unless you have to. Do not walk through water that is moving. Also, do not drive into flooded areas.

[ ] Floods can be very dangerous. However, if you are prepared, you will be able to act quickly and safely. Perhaps you haven't been in a flood yet, but it's always possible. Thank you!

B Plan your how-to speech about preparing for an emergency. Use the chart below to organize your thoughts.

How to Prepare for a ____________			
Step One	**Step Two**	**Step Three**	**Step Four**

C Now go to your notebook to write your own how-to speech about preparing for an emergency.

My writing checklist:

- ☐ I got all the information I needed for my speech.
- ☐ I organized the information into steps.
- ☐ I introduced the steps with words such as *first*, *next*, and *finally*.
- ☐ I included an introduction and a conclusion in my speech.

What did you learn?

BIG QUESTION 8
What can we learn from nature's power?

Review

destroyed sleeping bag funnel turned on
earthquake batteries snowfall canned food
tsunami landslide turned back supplies
bottled water tornado collapsed
flashlight rescue worker

A Unscramble the words.

1 ______________________
l h t f i h a s g l

2 ______________ ______________
t o l b d t e t a w r e

3 ______________ ______
g e n i s p l e g b a

4 ______________________
s i t e a b t r e

5 ______________ ______________
e u c r s e o k r w r e

6 ______________ ________
d n a c n e o f d o

7 ______________________
s p u e p l i s

B Complete the sentences with the words in the box.

1 An ______________ under the ocean can cause a ______________.

2 A ______________ often looks like a giant spinning ______________.

3 Fortunately, the hikers ______________ during the heavy rain and missed the ______________ that happened later on the hill.

4 The ______________ was so heavy that some roofs ______________.

C **Rewrite the sentences using *already*, *just*, or *yet*. If possible, use short forms with the subject pronouns.**

1 She has brought the first-aid kits to the storm shelter. × ⊗ | ×

2 We haven't had a big thunderstorm this summer. × × | ⊗

3 The hurricane is fast. It has made landfall. ⊗ × | ×

4 They haven't shown good teamwork. × × | ⊗

5 He has turned up the radio to hear the news. × ⊗ | ×

D **Rewrite each sentence and add *ever*. Turn the underlined word into an adverb of manner that ends in *-ly*.**

1 Have you seen a tornado spinning vertical across the ground?

2 Has the bodyguard protected the singer quick during an earthquake?

3 Has he seen this river rising slow until it became a flood?

4 Have raindrops fallen loud on this metal roof?

5 Have these power lines shaken violent during a hurricane?

BIG QUESTION 9

Why are biomes important?

Think and write.

What do you know?

What do you want to know?

Words

A Look and write.

tropical rainforest	tundra	cactus	desert
freshwater	sloth	temperate forest	grassland

1 

2 

3 

4 

5 

6 

7 

8 

B Circle the correct words.

1 The **tundra** / **grassland** biome is always frozen.

2 A **sloth** / **cactus** lives easily without much water.

3 The **temperate forest** / **taiga** biome has evergreen trees.

4 A **desert** / **tropical rainforest** is the driest biome on Earth.

5 There may be new medicines to be discovered in a **tropical rainforest** / **sloth**.

6 You might find a zebra or a rhinoceros in the **grassland** / **temperate forest**.

C Complete the sentences. Use the word pairs in the box.

desert–cactuses   freshwater–biomes   taiga–temperate forest   tundra–equator   tropical rainforest–sloth

1 If you hike through a ____________, you may see a ____________ hanging quietly from a tree branch.

2 Both the ocean and ____________ are water ____________, but the ocean is much larger.

3 A dry ____________ may have ____________ that are up to twenty meters tall.

4 The cold ____________ is far from the ____________, which is around the middle of Earth.

5 Tree-loving squirrels can be found in both the ____________ and the ____________.

Student Book page 168

Read

A Read. Why is it important to protect biomes?

B Read again. As you read, try to classify and categorize the information into groups.

Our Disappearing Biomes

Biomes are natural communities of plants and animals that live together in different places on Earth. People have used these biomes for food, water, and shelter for a very long time. However, some parts of biomes are beginning to disappear. People are using too many of the things biomes provide.

Tropical rainforests cover many areas near the earth's **equator**. They give Earth oxygen and help take away carbon dioxide. Half of all the plant and animal groups in the world live in tropical rainforests. The plants in this biome may give us new medicines, so scientists often travel to tropical rainforests to study these plants. However, many people have cut down the trees. They use the rainforest for farmland. Sadly, half of the world's rainforests are now gone, and more disappear every day.

The **freshwater** biome is a biome that all living things need. It gives people water to drink and wash with. Many animals also drink this water or live in it. However, people are using more and more freshwater in cities and on farms. Many rivers and lakes have less water now.

Think
In what ways do rainforests and freshwater help people?

Grasslands often have flowers, which are good for bees. These bees help plants to make new plants. Grassland plants also have deep roots. This keeps the soil strong. However, people are turning many grasslands into farmland. Some of the farmland soil blows away. Some of it washes into rivers.

Oceans, **temperate forests**, the **taiga**, and the **tundra** are also in trouble. When people take too many things from biomes, animals and plants there start to disappear.

Think
Which biome contains bees? Which contains drinking water?

People need biomes for many reasons. It is important to protect them while we use them. Fortunately, people are working hard to protect biomes. Without biomes, many plants and animals would leave the world forever.

Student Book page 169

Understand

Comprehension

A **Which biome would you like to visit and learn more about? Write about which biome you want to visit and two things you want to learn about that biome.**

____

____

B **Match each sentence to its group.**

~~1~~ It gives us oxygen, which we need to live.

2 It gives us water to drink.

3 It is good for bees, which help plants to make new plants.

4 It has plants that may give us new medicines.

5 It has plants that keep the soil strong.

6 It gives us water to wash with.

Tropical Rainforest	Grassland	Freshwater
1		

C **Answer the questions.**

1 What do rainforests help take away from us?

____

2 What happens to some farmland soil?

____

3 What happens when people take too many things from biomes?

____

D **Words in Context** Read and write.

Arctic	hatches	glides	scenes

1 This desert snake ____________ from an egg.

2 An eagle often ____________ in the sky, searching for animals below.

3 Some ____________ in a tropical rainforest may include sloths in trees.

4 The ____________ fox lives in the tundra along with the polar bear.

Grammar in Use

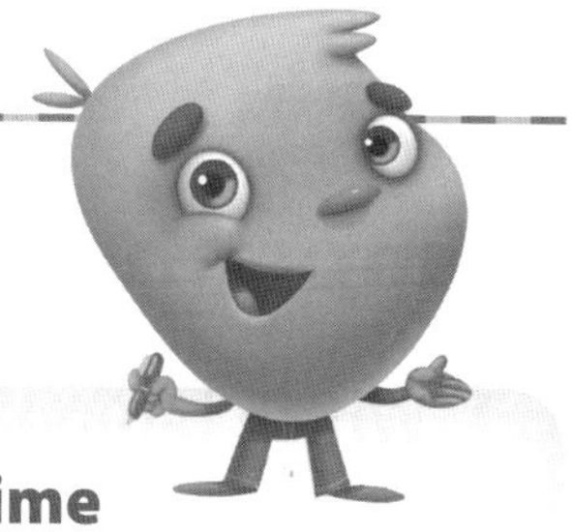

A Study the grammar.

Learn **Present Perfect with *For* and *Since***

Period of Time	Point in Time
People **have used** these biomes for food, water, and shelter ***for*** a very long time.	Pollution **has hurt** biomes in our area ***since*** I was a child.
Scientists **haven't seen** a living golden toad ***for*** over twenty years.	People in many countries **haven't hunted** whales ***since*** 1982.

B **Change the tense of the underlined verb. Then complete the sentence with *for* or *since*.**

1 Antonio hasn't ~~bike~~ hiked in a rainforest **since** he was in high school.

2 The camels haven't drink water on this desert journey __________ three days.

3 The people of the tundra have eat seal meat __________ a long time.

4 Unfortunately, our city zoo hasn't have sloths __________ 2005.

5 Ja-hoon has travel to the equator twice __________ he became a biologist.

6 Grasslands have be a safe home for many animals __________ centuries.

7 Maria's grandfather has go fishing in this lake __________ over thirty years.

8 People haven't take trees from this forest __________ they passed the new law.

9 Scientists have find new plants in the rainforest __________ many years.

10 My father hasn't visit Russia __________ he moved to New York.

C Complete the sentences with the phrases in the box and *for* or *since*.

hundreds of years   this morning   1987   two weeks

1 Clara and her classmates have studied biomes ______________________.

2 I haven't seen a cactus on this hike ______________________.

3 Our government has protected this rainforest ______________________.

4 Polar bears have lived in this part of the tundra ______________________.

D Cross out the wrong word. Then rewrite the sentence to make it correct.

1 Sonya has lived in the taiga since two years.

____

2 We haven't sail on the ocean since 2008.

____

3 This sloth have slept for twelve hours.

____

4 The scientist hasn't visit the tundra since last summer.

____

E Read. Then write a *how long*? question for each statement.

1 Elephants have lived in this grassland for centuries.

How long have elephants lived in this grassland?

2 They have studied biomes since last Wednesday.

____

3 Seals have swum along this coast for a long time.

____

Communicate

Word Study

catch stitch scratch patch itch batch

A **Circle the correct *-tch* word for each sentence.**

1 The president has received a **stitch** / **batch** of letters about protecting our biomes.

2 You can **catch** / **patch** a cold in the desert as well as in the tundra.

3 After the rainforest hike I **scratched** / **stitched** my sock because it had a hole in the toe.

4 The mother sloth **scratched** / **itched** her baby's back.

5 The polar bear rolled on the ice because its back **stitched / itched.**

6 Lassi selected an open **patch** / **batch** in the taiga to grow a vegetable garden.

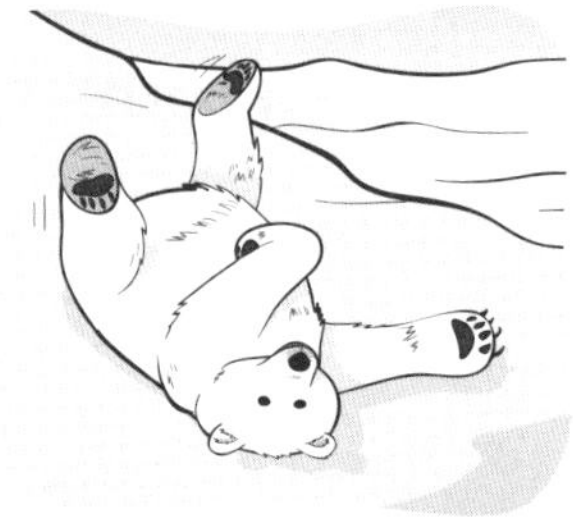

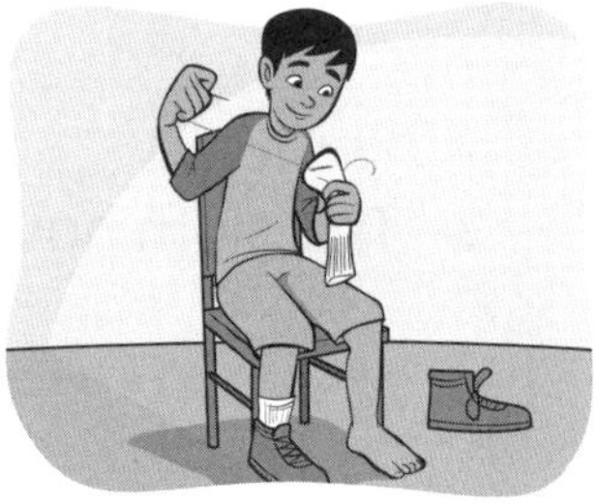

B **Complete the sentences with the words in the box.**

Omar's desert hike was very interesting. He saw a large bird ________ (1) a snake! However, he had a few problems. First, his shirt made his back ________ (2), so he had to ________ (3) it with a stick he found on the ground. At lunch, he had to ________ (4) his backpack with thread, because there was a hole in it. Fortunately, his guide was very kind. He brought a ________ (5) of cookies to eat on the hike. Then he took Omar to a ________ (6) of the desert that had some trees to sit under.

Writing Study

A **Combine the two sentences with the word *until*. Use pronouns if possible.**

1 The biologists found a sloth. The biologists hiked through the tropical rainforest.

The biologists hiked through the tropical rainforest until they found a sloth.

2 The lion ran through the grassland. The lion caught the zebra.

3 The freshwater reached the ocean. The freshwater flowed through the river.

4 The temperate forest ground was covered with leaves. The leaves fell from the trees.

5 The whale swam through the Pacific Ocean. The whale reached Hawaii.

B **Read. Then write a paragraph about someone who visits a biome. Write at least one present perfect sentence with *for* or *since*. Write at least one sentence combining two actions with *until*.**

Ahmad **has studied** the rainforest **since September**. Tomorrow he will hike through a real rainforest with his father near the Congo River in Africa. They will hike there **until** Ahmad's school holiday ends next Sunday. Ahmad **has thought** about this trip **for a long time**!

Words

petition seahorse astonish border marine park
parrot fish speedboat law sea turtle snorkel manta ray

A **Read and write.**

1 ______________________ 4 ______________________

2 ______________________ 5 ______________________

3 ______________________ 6 ______________________

B **Write. Change the verb tense if necessary.**

Too many speedboats were coming near the ________(1). Many people signed a ________(2), asking the government to keep the boats far away. The number of signatures ________(3) the people in the government. They passed a new ________(4) that kept the speedboats far away from the marine park.

C Circle the correct word. Then match.

1 The **manta ray** / **seahorse** gets its name from an animal that people ride.

2 The **parrot fish** / **sea turtle** is named after a colorful bird that lives in tropical areas.

3 People often **snorkel** / **astonish** together to see the beautiful coral and fish.

4 Rivers are natural **marine parks** / **borders** that often separate countries.

5 People can sign a **law** / **petition** to save the sea turtles if they want to.

6 As they snorkeled, they could hear the **speedboat** / **seahorse** in the water.

☐ 

☐ 

☐ 

☐ 

☐ 

☐ 

D Complete the sentences with the word pairs in the box.

law–border snorkeled–astonished marine park–parrot fish
sea turtle–seahorse manta ray–speedboat

1 An adult ______________________ is much bigger than a ______________________.

2 As we ______________________, the colors of the coral and fish nearby ______________________ us.

3 The ______________________ swam away as it heard the noisy ______________________ coming near.

4 The ______________________ has so many colorful ______________________ swimming around in it.

5 A new ______________________ has moved the eastern ______________________ of this marine park ten kilometers farther from the coast.

A Read. How do people harm forests?

B Read again. As you read, ask yourself open-ended questions to understand the story better.

Bruno's Dream

Bruno Serrano was a nine-year-old boy from São Paulo, Brazil. His mother, Beatriz, was a high school teacher. She taught Bruno to **snorkel** when he was six years old. A year later, she took him on a **speedboat** to see the beautiful Iguazu Falls of Brazil and Argentina.

São Paulo is in an area called the Atlantic Forest. This area stretches from the eastern tip of Brazil to Paraguay and Argentina. Bruno loved hiking in the forest more than anything. The different plants and animals **astonished** him, and he enjoyed spending time deep in the forest. However, Bruno's mother told him that about eighty percent of the original forest was gone. People removed many of the trees and sold them. They turned the forest into farms. Every year more of the forest disappeared. The forest was shrinking quickly.

One day Bruno was hiking with his mother in the forest when they saw large machines cutting down trees. He watched as a beautiful, enormous, old tree fell to the ground with a loud boom.

"Oh, no! They're destroying the forest!" shouted Bruno. "How can they do that?"

"They're outside of the park **border**," his mother explained. "Unfortunately, we can't do anything to stop them."

Think Ask yourself an open-ended question about forests.

"I have to do something," said Bruno. "We've hiked here since I was little."

Back in São Paulo, Bruno started a **petition** at his school. It asked the government to help save the Atlantic Forest. Students from other schools heard about Bruno's petition. Hundreds of children signed it. Bruno then sent it to the city council of São Paulo. Soon a new **law** kept more of the forest safe around the city.

"It's my dream to protect all of the Atlantic Forest someday," said Bruno.

Think Ask yourself an open-ended question about petitions.

"Don't give up, and your dream will come true," said his mother.

Student Book page 177

Understand

Comprehension

A **Would you do the same thing as Bruno? Why or why not? Write your answer and reasons.**

____

____

B **Match each open-ended question to two possible answers.**

1 How did Bruno's mother help Bruno to care about nature?

2 Why did the government pass the new law in São Paulo?

a She explained to Bruno how the forest was quickly disappearing.

b The city council knew that healthy forests are important for the world.

c She took Bruno out to see Brazil's beautiful nature up close.

d The city council knew that the children of São Paulo wanted to protect the forest.

C **Answer the questions.**

1 What two countries share the Iguazu Falls?

____

2 How did Bruno help save the Atlantic Forest?

____

3 What is Bruno's dream?

____

D **Words in Context** **Read and write.**

managed	invited	signed	difference

1 The city council ______________ Bruno to City Hall.

2 Bruno made a ______________ by starting a petition.

3 Bruno's teachers ______________ his petition, too.

4 The park staff ______________ part of the Atlantic Forest.

Student Book page 180

Grammar in Use

A Study the grammar.

Learn Present Perfect and Simple Past

Present Perfect	Simple Past
We **have studied** biomes before.	We **studied** biomes last week.
I **haven't hiked** in a long time.	I **didn't hike** this morning.
Have you **seen** a rainforest yet?	**Did** you **see** a rainforest last year?

B Circle the best tense for each sentence below.

1 **Did you study / Have you studied** the rainforest last year?
Yes, I **have / did**. I **studied / have studied** about it last December.

2 I **never saw / have never seen** a real shark in the ocean.
I'm glad I **haven't / didn't**!

3 Sue **has already snorkeled / already snorkeled** in the coral reef.
She **has done it / did it** this morning.

4 Michael **hasn't signed / didn't sign** the petition yet.
He thought he **has signed / signed** it yesterday.

5 **Have / Did** scientists ever **find / found** new kinds of fish in this marine park?
Of course! In fact, they **have found / found** three new kinds last month.

6 Tim **worked / has worked** at the marine park since April.
He **has never worked / never worked** at a zoo.

C Match.

1 I snorkeled at Glover's Reef •
2 I haven't snorkeled at all •

• a since last summer.
• b last summer.

3 Sea turtles haven't ever •
4 Sea turtles didn't •

• c laid eggs on this beach.
• d lay eggs on this beach last May.

5 This marine park protected •
6 This marine park hasn't protected •

• e its coral reefs well.
• f its coral reefs well last year.

D Complete the sentences with *did*, *have*, or *has*, and the verb in parentheses. Change the tense of the verb if necessary.

1 __Has__ Fred __seen__ (see) any sea turtles in the ocean yet?

2 I ________ just ________ (swim) with two sea turtles! It was amazing!

3 ________ Maria ________ (ride) on the speedboat last night?

4 ________ they ever ________ (change) the borders of this marine park?

E Use the prompts to change each sentence from present perfect to simple past.

1 The seahorses haven't come to this area yet. (last year)

__The seahorses didn't come to this area last year.__

2 The speedboat has already left the area. (five minutes ago)

____

3 The members of the city council haven't received the petition. (this morning)

____

4 Have they snorkeled around the marine park yet? (yesterday)

____

Word Study

independent	independence	absent	absence	intelligent	intelligence

A Complete each word with the suffix *-ent* or *-ence*. Then number.

1 Elephants, dolphins, and chimpanzees are some of the most intellig_______ animals in the world. Their intellig_______ has astonished scientists.

2 A leopard shows a lot of independ_______. For example, you will usually see it hunting alone. Leopards are very independ_______ compared to other big cats.

3 When the rainforest hike was over, Jerome was abs_______ from the group. His abs_______ worried the guides. However, they found him taking pictures of a sloth.

B Complete the sentences with words from the box.

1 The _______________ of speedboats in this area is wonderful. We can snorkel in peace and quiet. It's too bad that Jen is _______________ from our group today.

2 The Portia Labiata Jumping Spider has so much _______________. It is called the smartest bug in the world. I wonder if other spiders are that _______________?

3 Sea turtles are quite _______________. They usually swim alone. This _______________ makes it difficult for people to see them easily.

Writing Study

A **Combine the sentences using *since* or *because*. Use pronouns if possible.**

1 The Atlantic Forest is disappearing. People are cutting down the trees.

The Atlantic Forest is disappearing because people are cutting down the trees.

2 Biomes are important. Biomes keep our planet healthy.

3 Speedboats scare fish away. Speedboats are bad for coral reefs.

4 This fish is called a seahorse. A seahorse looks like a tiny horse.

5 Some people hurt biomes. We need laws to protect biomes.

B **Write a paragraph about why we need to protect biomes. Write at least one sentence in the simple past and one in the present perfect. Write at least one sentence that combines two actions with *since* or *because*.**

Yesterday I **snorkeled** in the ocean. I saw beautiful fish swimming around the coral. Coral reefs **have been** endangered for a long time. We need to protect them **since** so many important plants and animals live there. Coral reefs keep oceans healthy.

Writing

A Read this fictional story about a girl who visits her grandfather in the taiga of Finland. Label the parts of the story.

The Last Picture

Sini woke up to the sound of birds in the trees. She was spending a week with her grandfather in the taiga of Finland.

"Good morning!" her grandfather said. "After breakfast, we'll hike through the forest. Don't forget your camera." Sini wanted to take a picture of a moose before she returned home.

While they were hiking, Sini heard a splash behind her. She turned to see a brown bear on the other side of a small lake. She quickly took its picture.

For six days Sini fished and hiked with her grandfather. She took many pictures. However, no moose appeared.

On her final day, Sini and her grandfather went fishing for the last time. Her grandfather fell asleep, but he woke up to Sini's voice.

"Be very quiet, Grandpa," she said. She pointed the camera toward him and took a picture.

"I'm sorry you haven't seen a moose," her grandfather said.

Sini pointed proudly to her camera. There in the picture, far behind her grandfather, was a large moose. Sini's last picture in the taiga was the best of all!

B Plan your fictional story. Use the chart to organize your ideas.

Setting (biome)	Characters	Conflict	Resolution

C Now go to your notebook to write your own story about someone living in a biome.

My writing checklist:

- ☐ I wrote a title for the story.
- ☐ I let the reader know the setting of the story.
- ☐ I created interesting characters with natural dialogue.
- ☐ I added a conflict to the plot. I resolved this conflict by the end of the story.
- ☐ I used descriptive language to create a strong image in the reader's mind.

Student Book page 184

What did you learn?

BIG QUESTION 9

Why are biomes important?

Review

Arctic	grassland	marine parks	sea turtles
temperate forest	desert	difference	parrot fish
tropical rainforest	freshwater	laws	tundra

A **Read and write.**

Biomes

Biomes are natural communities of plants and animals. One kind of biome is the ocean. The colorful ____________ (1) lives there. In the ocean there are also ____________ (2), but they breathe air.

There are other biomes in the world, too. There is the ____________ (3) biome, which has almost no salt in the water. There is the ____________ (4), where polar bears and seals live. This biome is in the ____________ (5) region. There is the ____________ (6), with its snakes and cactuses. Elephants live in the African ____________ (7). In the ____________ (8), you may see a sloth in a tree. The ____________ (9) is another forest biome with rabbits, bears, and deer.

Fortunately, many countries have created ____________ (10) that protect biomes. Land parks and ____________ (11) are places where animals and plants are safe. When people try to protect biomes, they make an important ____________ (12) in our world.

B **Complete each sentence using *for* or *since*. Then change the sentence from present perfect to simple past.**

1 People in the tundra have eaten seal meat __for__ centuries. (in the 20th century)

People in the tundra ate seal meat in the 20th century.

2 People haven't hunted elephants in this grassland ________ 1973. (in 1974)

____

3 Sea turtles have laid eggs on this beach ________ fifty years. (last year)

____

____

4 The sloth hasn't moved in the tree ________ last night. (this morning)

____

____

C **Read. Then combine the two sentences using the word *until*. Use pronouns if possible.**

1 The students continued to sign petitions. The government passed the law.

____

2 The parrot fish swam away. Ken took pictures of the parrot fish.

____

3 The speedboat moved quickly. The speedboat reached the border of the marine park.

____

D **Combine the sentences. Write *since* or *because* in front of the reason. Use pronouns if possible.**

1 The government managed the taiga. People were cutting down too many trees.

____

2 The baby's back itched. The mother sloth scratched the baby's back.

____

3 Biomes keep our planet healthy. People need biomes.

____

Writing Process Steps

STEP 1: Brainstorm Ideas

- Think of what you want to write about. Write down all the ideas that come into your mind.
- Write as many ideas as you can. You don't have to use all of these ideas.

STEP 2: Organize Your Ideas

- Put your ideas into groups. Each group will be a paragraph in the body of your writing.
- Decide how many body paragraphs you will have.

STEP 3: Write Your Paragraphs

- Write an introduction paragraph. This should grab the reader's attention and introduce your topic.
- For each body paragraph, write a topic sentence. This tells the reader what a paragraph is about. Then write three or four sentences that support your topic sentence. Repeat this process for each body paragraph.
- Write a conclusion paragraph. This should summarize your main idea(s) and end with a strong, final thought.

STEP 4: Revise Your Work

- After you write your introduction, body, and conclusion paragraphs, read them again.
- Ask yourself: *Are my topic sentences clear? Are my supporting sentences strong and in the correct order? Did I use correct grammar and spell all my words correctly?*
- Then rewrite or correct parts of your writing that need more work.

Brainstorming and Organizing

Use graphic organizers like these to organize your ideas before writing.

What happened?
Who was there?
Why did it happen?
When did it happen?
Where did it happen?

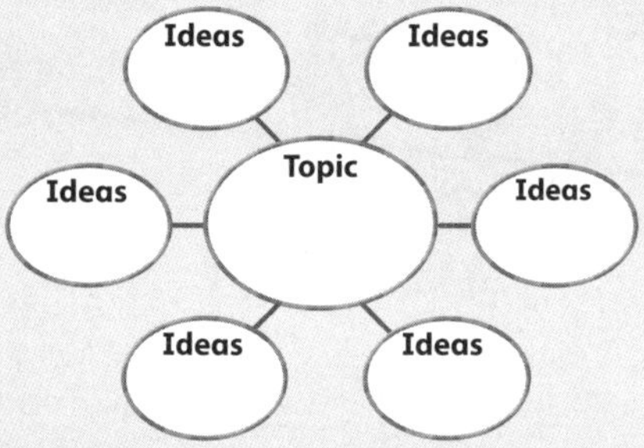

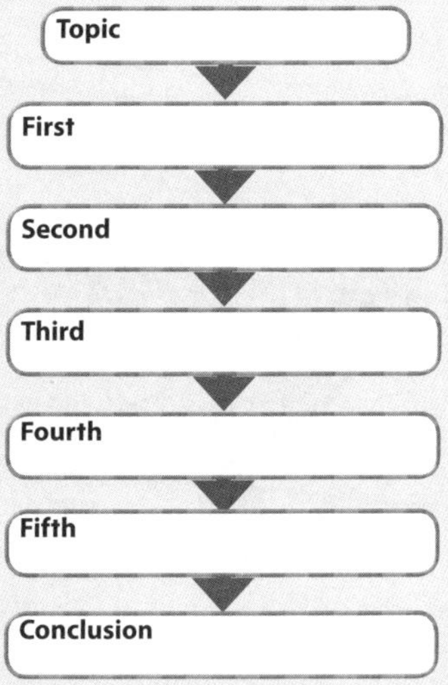

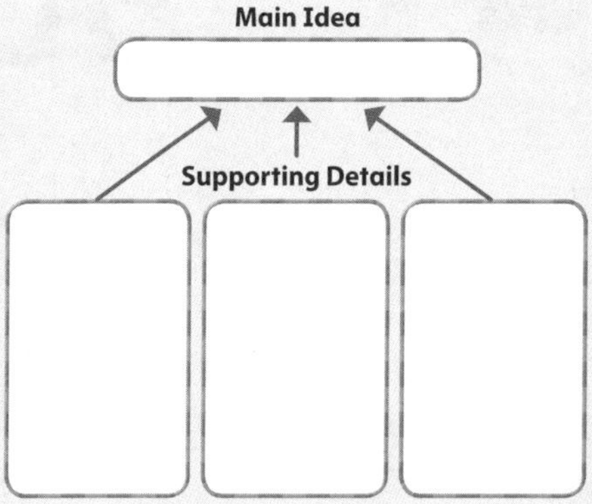

Parts of Speech

Part of Speech	Description	Examples
Verb	an action	I **like** to **work**. She **is singing**.
Noun	a person, place, or thing	**Tim** is my **friend**. The **school** is in **London**.
Adjective	describes a noun	I have **two** trees. The trees are **big**.
Adverb	describes a verb, an adjective, or an adverb	Jen runs **quickly**. Meg works **quietly**.
Pronoun	replaces a noun	**She** wants a snack. **It** looks great!
Preposition	links a noun to a location or to another word	The bookstore is **up** the street. We went to school **on** Monday.
Conjunction	joins parts of sentences or words	I like fruit, **and** I like vegetables. I like fruit, **but** I don't like vegetables.

Regular and Irregular Verbs

Learn Regular Verbs

Most verbs are regular. Add *-ed* to form the past tense of regular verbs.

We walk**ed** to the park.
John creat**ed** a new story.

Base Verb	Simple Past	Past Participle
be	was, were	been
become	became	become
begin	began	begun
break	broke	broken
bring	brought	brought
build	built	built
buy	bought	bought
catch	caught	caught
choose	chose	chosen
come	came	come
cut	cut	cut
do	did	done
drink	drank	drunk
drive	drove	driven
eat	ate	eaten
fall	fell	fallen
feel	felt	felt
find	found	found
fly	flew	flown
forget	forgot	forgotten
get	got	gotten
give	gave	given
go	went	gone
grow	grew	grown
have	had	had
hear	heard	heard
hold	held	held
hurt	hurt	hurt
keep	kept	kept
know	knew	known

Learn Irregular Verbs

Some verbs are irregular. We don't use *-ed* to form the past tense. We have to learn the past tense form of each verb. For tenses such as the present perfect, you have to learn the past participle form.

Base Verb	Simple Past	Past Participle
leave	left	left
let	let	let
lose	lost	lost
make	made	made
meet	met	met
pay	paid	paid
read	read	read
ride	rode	ridden
run	ran	run
say	said	said
see	saw	seen
sell	sold	sold
send	sent	sent
sing	sang	sung
sit	sat	sat
sleep	slept	slept
speak	spoke	spoken
spend	spent	spent
stand	stood	stood
swim	swam	swum
take	took	taken
teach	taught	taught
tell	told	told
think	thought	thought
throw	threw	thrown
understand	understood	understood
wake	woke	woken
wear	wore	worn
win	won	won
write	wrote	written

Verb Tenses

Present

Learn Simple Present

Use the simple present for things that happen regularly.

I **eat** dinner at 6 p.m.
She **plays** basketball.

Learn Present Continuous

Use the present continuous for things that are happening right now or to talk about future plans.

He **is playing** the violin.
They **are going** to Paris next year.

Learn Present Perfect

Use the present perfect for past experiences, past actions that continue to the present, or actions that happened at an unknown time.

I **have thrown** a baseball.
She **has lived** here for a long time.
They **have** never **visited** a volcano.

Past

Learn Simple Past

Use the simple past for things that happened in the past, especially at a specific time.

He **played** tennis yesterday.
They **went** to a concert last night.

Learn Past Continous

Use the past continuous for what was going on during a time in the past.

I **was eating** breakfast.
She **was playing** in the park.

Future

Learn Simple Future

Use the simple future for future facts, plans to do something, or predictions.

I **will eat** dinner at 6 p.m.
He **will play** soccer tomorrow.
They **will win** the game.

Conditionals

Learn Present Real Conditional

Use the present real conditional for something that happens and causes another thing to happen.

If I **am hungry**, I **eat** a snack.
When she **is bored**, she **plays** a game.

Learn Future Real Conditional

Use the future real conditional for future possibilities and what will happen as a result.

If I **go** to the store, I **will buy** some snacks.
If he **visits** the museum, he **will see** exhibits.